CORNISH
TALES OF MYSTERY
AND MURDER

Other titles in this series include:

CORNISH TALES OF MYSTERY AND MURDER

Sheila Bird

COUNTRYSIDE BOOKS
NEWBURY BERKSHIRE

First published 2002
© Sheila Bird 2002

COUNTRYSIDE BOOKS
3 Catherine Road
Newbury, Berkshire

To view our complete range of books,
please visit us at
www.countrysidebooks.co.uk

ISBN 1 85306 747 4

Produced through MRM Associates Ltd., Reading
Printed by J. W. Arrowsmith Ltd., Bristol

Contents

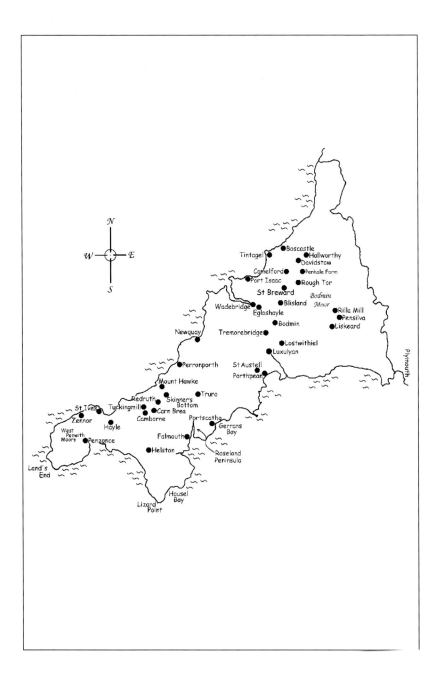

A SPOOKY WARTIME
LEGACY AT HOUSEL BAY

During the Second World War, when a large percentage of the young and fit were conscripted into the services, those who found themselves at the RAF base close to Lizard Point counted themselves very lucky, for they were billeted in the commandeered hotel complex at Housel Bay, with stunning coastal views and the opportunity to enjoy swinging parties on the beach below. At this time of uncertainty, everyone was aware of the possibility of an early death at the hands of the enemy, but no one would have foreseen, in this heavenly setting, the fate of a beautiful, vivacious, dark-haired WAAF from Porthcawl and a Flying Officer from Bath.

As dawn broke over the Lizard on a moist and silvery late October morning in 1943, the sound of a shot set the seagulls wheeling and protesting. This was followed by a second shot a few moments later, and William Croft, the Station Commander, emerged from the wooden summerhouse situated in the hotel's lovely gardens which sloped down to the sea. Six days later, on 22nd October, the *Falmouth Packet* reported that Flying Officer William James Croft, aged 32, a married man with two children, had been brought before magistrates in Helston on the previous Saturday night, on a charge of wilfully murdering Joan Nora Lewis, aged 27. He had been remanded for 21 days and taken to Exeter Prison the next day.

Corporal Joan Lewis had been serving at Housel Bay for some time before Croft arrived on the scene as Commanding Officer.

Housel Bay Hotel, designed by Silvanus Trevail, became the scene of a crime of passion during the Second World War. (Taken with kind permission of the Housel Bay Hotel)

Having first encountered each other at a bathing party down on the beach, they found themselves thrown together in the course of their duties, and the agreeable friendship developed into a deep and passionate love affair. Croft, who had previously been an administrator for the GPO in Bristol, had a troubled conscience, not only on account of committing adultery, but also for breaking the service code of non-fraternisation between the ranks. Such qualms prompted him to confide in the officer in charge of the WAAFS, who were quartered in the main hotel building. She told him that she did not approve of the association, and that it should cease. Next day Croft told his lover that they could not both remain at the same station, and, as Headquarters would not agree to the Flying Officer being moved, this resulted in arrangements being made for Joan Lewis to be transferred to a station in Devon on Saturday, 16th October. However, the prospect of being parted was too painful to contemplate, and in one of many letters to her Croft had written, 'The thought of some other male sharing your company drives me to distraction. Please don't let us think of Saturday, Joan darling. I cannot dare to think of it. Every time, I get a horrible aching pain.'

Lewis took a couple of days' leave, which she spent with Croft, and returned to duty on the 14th. She seemed to be quite cheerful in her interaction with everybody the next day, and the lovers apparently spent most of that night in the summerhouse. Had she realised that she would never see another dawn? Perhaps the star-crossed lovers had planned to meet in Paradise, in the traditional style of tragi-romanticism.

According to initial reports, after the shooting Flying Officer Croft had telephoned another officer, urging him to come to the summerhouse right away, and was overheard saying, 'I have killed Joan Lewis.' Then Flying Officer Norman Page and a sergeant climbed through the summerhouse window and discovered the body of the woman, which had slumped from a seat and onto the floor, where it lay in a pool of blood. There was a service revolver on a table, containing four live rounds and two empty cartridge cases. Croft asked his fellow officer to inform the police, then said that he and the girl had decided to finish it all, but when it came to it he had not had the courage to shoot himself.

Throughout the entire investigation Croft insisted many times that Joan had fired both shots. When initially charged with the murder he replied, 'I did not murder Joan Lewis. She shot herself twice. The first time was in the left of her chest. I do not know where the other wound was. We had both agreed to commit suicide.' He said the arrangement was that they would shoot themselves, one after the other, with the same revolver.

Dr Hocking, the county pathologist, said that Lewis had been shot twice: first through the left side of her chest near her heart, then on the left side of her head. The chest wound would have been inflicted whilst she was sitting on the settee, as indicated by a bloodstained bullet hole in the back of the settee, from which a flattened bullet was later extracted. This shot would have been fired about five or six inches from her chest and was probably aimed at her heart, but it would not have been fatal. The massive amount of bleeding from this area, which would only occur when the blood vessels were still under pressure from the heart, demonstrated that she was still alive after this shot, whereas the subsequent head injury would have caused instantaneous death. The revolver on the nearby table had been fired, but the firing pin had struck a third shell, which had not fired, and remained in position in the chamber.

Croft was committed for trial at the Winchester Assizes the following month. At the trial it was the submission of the prosecution that it was quite impossible for the girl to have shot herself twice. When charged with the murder Croft was alleged to have replied, 'At this stage all I wish to say is I did not murder Joan Lewis. She shot herself twice. We had both agreed to commit suicide.' After evidence had been given, Croft entered the dock and said, 'I am not guilty. I did not kill Joan Lewis. She shot herself. That is all. I do not wish to give any evidence at this stage. I reserve my defence.'

Flying Officer Norman Page described how he and a sergeant had climbed through the window of the summerhouse and seen the body of Corporal Joan Lewis. PC Leslie Jones and Superintendent Thomas Morcumb of Falmouth also gave evidence. Croft allegedly told Morcumb, 'Not murder, Sir. I was there. It is my coat and revolver. I have a full statement to make, but I do not want to say anything until I have had advice from Headquarters.' Sergeant Stone of Helston Police told the jury that after being cautioned the accused said, 'I want to express the feeling I had at the time this affair happened. It's horrible; it comes over me very occasionally. I feel as though a wheel is spinning in my head at a terrific speed, which tries to lift me, and then I am not master of myself. I am dazed or paralysed, and then it subsides very quickly. I am saying this as it is a relief to get it off my mind.'

At the trial it was stated that acquaintance had ripened into love, but the potentially scandalous situation had become well nigh intolerable. When it came to the point of Joan Lewis being posted to another station they felt they could not face it and discussed suicide. Describing their last night together, Croft said that he fetched a revolver from his office, loaded it, and met his lover in the summerhouse. She felt the weight of the revolver in the pocket of his great coat, and they sat and smoked, then dozed. She awakened him at 2.30 am, when they should have gone back to the hotel, but they did not want to go. They awoke again at 4.30, and he said that it was time they were moving. 'I could not possibly explain my feelings at the time,' he told the court. 'There was a moon, but the light was obscured by clouds. We could just distinguish each other. It was raining heavily and blowing a gale. I placed the gun on our laps. We placed our hands together after I had got the revolver. We sat like that for some considerable time. I felt Joan's hand leave mine, and the weight of the revolver was taken off my knee. The next thing, I heard a shot. He said he leapt up and the girl cried, 'Fetch some help quickly. It is hurting me.' He asked her where it was hurting, and she said, 'In my chest.' Croft stated that he opened a window and climbed out from the summerhouse, and after a few paces he heard a second shot. He said that he took the pistol intending to shoot himself, but he could not do it. He went on to explain that when he had told Page that he had killed Joan Lewis, he meant that he felt himself responsible for what had happened, not that he had actually physically killed her.

Mr Maude KC, counsel for the prosecution, read out a number of Croft and Lewis's letters, which were of a passionate nature, and said there was no doubt they were in love. 'This man, either because he was jealous, or feared that he would no longer be able to possess the girl – as no doubt he had possessed her for several months – or for some other reason, having decided possibly on suicide, had the courage to kill her, but lacked it to kill himself.' There was a touch of drama in the courtroom when two revolvers were produced. One was held by Dr Hocking, the pathologist, and the other by the counsel for the defence. Dr Hocking was giving evidence based on the tests he had made in reconstructing what had happened in the summerhouse. To illustrate this, he went through the contortions in the witness box that would have been necessary for Joan to have achieved a suicidal shot. The counsel for the defence was focusing attention on the head wound, inflicted by the second shot. He demonstrated his line of argument by dropping his elbow on the table to show that the force could have played a part in causing the revolver to go off. The counsel suggested to Dr Hocking that if the pistol went off as the woman fell, still clutching it, the bullet would have flown upwards through her head. The pathologist said that she would have had to turn her head around. His response to an earlier question, as to whether it was possible for a revolver to be used by someone already injured, had been that it was very unlikely.

The question of suicide was thought to be crucial to the outcome of the case. Mr Maude repeated Hocking's view that it was improbable that the woman could have put a bullet into herself, and then have been able to hold the revolver steadily at some distance in order to shoot herself through the head. Counsel for the defence pointed out that the first shot did not kill the girl; the second shot did, but it was not fired in carrying out their agreement to commit suicide. That agreement was over as soon as the first shot was fired; the shock of the first shot had brought Croft to his senses. Croft pleaded 'Not guilty'.

In summing up, the judge explained that suicide was self-murder, and if the girl had killed herself deliberately, by shooting herself, she had committed murder, and if the man were aiding and abetting her, he was as guilty of murder as if he himself had shot her. The jury took only 20 minutes to reach their verdict. Mr Justice Humphreys told Croft, 'The jury have convicted you on evidence which, in my opinion, leaves no room for doubt. . .' and he was sentenced to be hanged. However, not everyone agreed with these conclusions, and the case went to the Court of Criminal Appeal.

The main grounds of appeal were that the judge had misdirected the jury in not putting to them the possibility of its being an accident; that he had been wrong in telling them that the appellant must be presumed to have intended the obvious consequences of his act; that he had been wrong in saying that the appellant was guilty of murder merely because the alleged suicide was the result of an agreement between the appellant and the deceased; and that the possibility of manslaughter had not been put to them. Throughout the hearing learned minds were fully stretched, citing conflicting legal precedents and interpreting and reinterpreting legal definitions. Croft based his appeal on the ground of misdirection of the jury by the judge.

At the appeal the idea was put forward that the fatal shot had

VIGIL AT
HOUSEL BAY.

An artist's sketch of the ghostly WAAF, waiting for her lover in the garden.
(Courtesy of Derek Oswald, Housel Bay Hotel)

been fired by the the deceased woman in his absence, and therefore he should be acquitted. The interpretations of his story – that Joan took the revolver, discharged it while they were sitting together in the summerhouse, wounding herself in the left breast; in great pain, she begged him to summon help; he climbed out of the window and had taken a few paces towards the house when he heard another shot; returning to the summerhouse he discovered that she had accidentally or intentionally shot herself through the head – and their legal implications were kicked to and fro in the manner of some litigating football. It was contended that an agreement to commit suicide would not make the survivor guilty of counselling, advising or procuring or abetting, if he was not present when the suicide was committed. But if she had indeed fired the first shot, why did he scramble out of the window, leaving her with the revolver, instead of trying to persuade her not to take things any further? Did not the fact that she had asked for help indicate her desire to live, therefore ending the suicide pact? Croft had left Corporal Lewis wounded, possibly fatally, with a revolver loaded in all chambers except the one which had been fired.

The Court of Appeal did not consider that Croft had established that he had expressly countermanded or revoked the advising, counselling, procuring, or abetting which he had previously given, and thus could not escape being held guilty for what happened. His appeal was dismissed, but his sentence was reduced to life imprisonment, and he was in fact released a few years later.

An eerie sequel to this tragic wartime tale of love and overriding passion lingers on. When Commander T.E. Stanley and his wife bought the Housel Bay Hotel in 1978 they found that they were getting more for their money than they bargained for. The situation took on a new dimension when the couple wrote and told their friends, the Hockings, that the ghost of a young woman in WAAF uniform had been seen by a number of people on various occasions in the hotel gardens in the month of October. Local folk had told them that a girl was supposed to have been murdered by her lover when she was billeted there as a member of the WAAF radar plotting team in 1943.

In October 1978, an elderly lady of rather ample proportions from Stockport booked in for a short break, and not being of a very athletic build decided in favour of spending most of her time sitting reading in the garden, with her lap dog. On the second afternoon of her visit she arrived in the hotel reception area in a very distressed state, with tears streaming down her cheeks. They tried to calm her down, and when she had composed herself she explained that she was a medium, and while sitting on a seat in the lower part of the garden, she had heard the sound of a woman weeping. Realising that this was a spiritual encounter, she had entered into conversation with the invisible woman. The spirit said she was a young WAAF, waiting for her lover, who was also her murderer, to join her as he had promised when they made a suicide pact in 1943. The woman, who had never visited Cornwall before, said that she had made an arrangement to revisit the spot at 9 pm that evening. She asked the hotel owner to escort her there by torchlight, and return in 15 minutes to check her well-being without distracting her from her trance-like state. If all was well he was to return a quarter of an hour later to accompany her back to the hotel, using force if necessary. However, no firm tactics were required, and on her return the weeping woman wrote out a detailed account of her conversation with the spirit, including relevant dates, which turned out to be accurate. She did not attempt to capitalise on the situation, and was accepted as being genuine.

Although the manifestations had been associated with October, the month of the tragedy, it was not invariably so. When a couple from Sheffield arrived at the hotel in August 1979 there were more eerie happenings. The husband, who always carried a sketchbook around with him when he was on holiday, returned from the lower garden one afternoon and mentioned to the proprietor that he had seen a young lady dressed in RAF blue with a sad, faraway look in her eyes, sitting on a seat as if waiting for someone to join her. He made some disparaging remark about the silly trend of young people dressing in World War Two garb, saying he just could not understand why they did it. Was she staying at the hotel? He saw her again the following day and was just about to speak to her, but changed his mind and walked straight past. When he mentioned this second encounter to the proprietor, Commander Stanley went to take a look himself. But the bench seat was empty. He indulged in a little badinage with his guest about fantasies of pretty young girls sitting on benches, and people pulling other people's legs. However, the man insisted that he had seen her sitting on the seat, and said he would keep an eye open for her around the hotel. The next afternoon he reported that she was back again, but when Commander Stanley went out, again there was no sign of her. When he protested that he was being taken for a ride, he was promptly shown the sketchbook, in which the guest had depicted the girl on the bench.

Later, Derek Oswald and his family took over the hotel and have reported no further sightings of the tragic young corporal, presumably no longer waiting for her lover on the bench in the garden above Housel Bay.

THE CORNISH
SEA MONSTER

Ican remember it as if it were yesterday. I had met my brother at
Truro station in the early evening of Wednesday, 10th July 1985
and had driven on to Portscatho for an exhilarating walk along
the cliffs and the chance to catch up on the news of the last few
months. My brother is a coastal geomorphologist based in
Australia, carrying out research all over the world, and was
making one of his frequent visits to Britain.

This summer's day had been grey and misty, but the sun began
to break through as we traversed the lush and lovely lanes of the
Roseland peninsula, creating conditions of exceptional clarity as
we started walking southwards on the long straight section of the
coastal footpath towards Killigerran Head. At that time of the
evening the sun was to our right, highlighting the intensely blue
waters of Gerrans Bay, and the protective profile of Nare Head, to
the north-east. There was a silvery sheen on the surface of the
water, which was as smooth and calm as the sea could ever be. I
noticed one or two small fishing boats dotted across the bay, and
flocks of birds silhouetted against the sky.

At about 8 o'clock, when we were deep in conversation, my
brother suddenly shouted, 'Whatever's that?' and drew my
attention to an enormous sea creature with a long neck and very
large hump, some distance to the south, keeping close inshore on
this exceptionally high tide, and progressing rapidly towards us.
My first reaction was one of shock and surprise. It seemed like

something that had escaped from the pages of some children's storybook. Was I dreaming? No, I was not. This was really happening; the seemingly impossible was actually happening; this was reality. And in those first few seconds I became aware that I would have to realign my concept of reality.

We gained a greater appreciation of the creature's remarkable size as it came nearer and nearer, keeping close to the cliffs, and presenting the appearance of something distinctly primeval, moving swiftly and smoothly like a stately galleon. And then the penny dropped. This was the mysterious sea monster that fisherman George Vinnicombe and others had told me about, which has come to be known as Morgawr (an anagram of ragworm). 'It's Morgawr! It's Morgawr!' I cried excitedly. 'What is that you keep saying?' asked my brother, and I explained that there had been a number of sightings of a large, unidentified sea serpent in the locality of Falmouth Bay over the past few years. As my brother was trying to attract the attention of two elderly passers-by with binoculars, I noticed a seagull peel away from the rest of the flock and swoop down low over the monster's head, which was held proudly aloft, then gain height and disappear from the scene. There was no response from the creature, which continued on its purposeful straight course close to the shoreline. The four of us were standing on the clifftop near Pencabe Point and were able to observe it in detail as the sun was shining directly onto it. The other three were passing the binoculars around, but I declined the offer as I thought it might be distracting in the way that photographing precious moments can be, and did not take my eyes off the scene.

It was certainly a stylish mover, totally in harmony with its environment, and making very little impact on the calm surface of the water as it glided nearer and nearer with splendid swan-like grace. When it reached a point directly offshore, we found ourselves looking obliquely down on it from a distance of about 100 yards. It was a mottled grey colour, had a camel-like head, which was small in comparison with the rest of its bulk, large round saucer eyes and a softly curving area around the mouth, which was closed. I wondered whether it was aware of our presence, and whether it had ever seen human beings before. The head, at the top of a long, quite slender neck, was held at rather a pert angle, giving it a cute, endearing look, reminiscent of something out of Edward Lear's whimsical repertoire. It appeared to be gentle and benign, not a fearsome monster of the deep. It was in its element and I in mine, and if I had been in a small boat I think I might have approached it, rather than retreated. This privileged close-up experience has given me a very personal and protective feeling towards this strange species.

Viewed in profile, it had muscular areas at the base of the neck and to the rear of the hump, which may well have appeared as two smaller humps when seen from a lower angle. It was difficult to estimate its size from that distance, without anything in the vicinity to give it scale. But it would have been many times bigger than a giant leatherback turtle. The neck might well have protruded anything up to 6 feet above the surface of the water, and we thought that the trunk of the body was probably about 20 feet long. As it passed the point where we were standing, I suddenly became aware of a long tapering tail trailing out behind, just below the surface of the water, and a broad, flattish area just beyond the base of the trunk. The animal was not being propelled by the tail, which was neither moving from side to side nor undulating up and down. It was difficult to see where the tail ended, as it appeared dark green below the surface of the water, and left a long, diminishing ripple pattern of water in its wake. This elegant creature did not display any momentum in its movement, which was swift and efficient, and palaeontologists (fossil experts) later told me that this was because the creature would have had four businesslike paddles obscured from our view beneath the water.

Having progressed some distance beyond us, it started to submerge, creating a slight swirling movement as it gradually sank, vertically, like a submarine, with head still held high. I can clearly visualise the stages of the descent, and recall my disappointment that our encounter was about to end. At one point the head, long neck and hump were visible above the surface; then a section of neck and the head; then just the head. As the head disappeared, there was a slight movement of water where the huge creature had just been, and a few bubbles on the surface. But within a couple of seconds all became calm, and no one would ever have thought that a sea monster had made an appearance, and must still be lurking in the vicinity. We waited for half an hour or so, hoping that it might resurface for air, as anything with a lung system might do, but we never saw it again. Those out fishing in the bay were oblivious of the presence of this strange sea creature so close to them on that calm summer's evening.

My brother, being based in Australia, had never heard of the Cornish sea monster and suggested that I notify the local newspaper, as it was an important sighting, worthy of serious scientific investigation. But I was reluctant to do so because I was launching my first book, *Bygone Falmouth,* and did not want people to think I was seeking timely publicity. However, a jokey piece about Morgawr in the *Falmouth Packet* a few weeks later filled us with dismay, and I wrote in to place our sighting on record, pointing out that such flippancy discredits those who have had genuine sightings and holds back worthwhile research. When I was being interviewed about my new book on 'Afternoon Sou' West' at the BBC studios in Plymouth on 21st October that year, the conversation turned to Morgawr, and three people took advantage of the following phone-in to say that they had seen the same creature frolicking in the sea off Pendennis Point, Falmouth during those few days in July.

Soon after experiencing this sighting, I contacted various authorities, including palaeontologists in Lyme Regis in Dorset and Axmouth in Devon. They both knew exactly what I was talking about, showed me pictures, and told me that what I had seen was a descendant of the plesiosaurus, thought to have become extinct over 64 million years ago, but known by some to still be in existence. One declared, 'I would give my right arm to see what you saw!' Subsequent visits to the scene of the sighting near Portscatho highlighted the fact that a series of sharp, rocky reefs running out at right angles to the shore are exposed at low tide, and it seems incredible that such a large creature could have been swimming along so close to the cliffs. This prompted me to get in touch with the United Kingdom Hydrographic Office in Taunton, who sent me a print-out of the tidal curve for Falmouth on that day, showing that the height of the tide was between 2.6 and 3.5 metres from 19.00 to 21.00 that evening.

The author's impression of the sea creature seen at Portscatho, July 1985.

I was later to discover that several different types of sea serpent have been spotted off the Cornish coast over the centuries, and my attention was drawn to the following report in the *West Briton* of 1876: 'The sea serpent was caught alive in Gerrans Bay. Two of our fishermen were afloat overhauling their crab pots about 400–500 yards from the shore, when they discovered the serpent coiled about their floating cork [buoy]. Upon their approach it lifted its head and showed signs of defiance, upon which they struck it forcibly with an oar, which so far disabled it as to allow them to proceed with their work, after which they observed the serpent floating about near their boat. They pursued it, bringing it ashore yet alive for exhibition, soon after which it was killed on the rocks and most inconsiderately cast again in the sea.'

Unfortunately no description was given of this sea serpent, which must have been much smaller than the Nessie-like specimen that we saw. However, there have been dozens of reliable sightings of sea monsters of the type we saw in 1985, usually coinciding with particularly warm summers and calm conditions, coming right up to the present day. They might well migrate from southern waters.

Although the sea monster is usually associated with Falmouth Bay, its river estuaries and the Lizard, one of the best sightings occurred off the north Cornish coast on 1st May, 1935, during a heatwave. Mrs F.E. South, proprietress of a guest house in Port Isaac, was relaxing on the clifftop between Port Isaac and Port Quin at about 11 o'clock in the morning, when she saw what she initially took to be a very strange boat. 'It was a funny shape and extremely black,' she said, 'and I thought it rather unusual. The thing was about a quarter of a mile from where I was sitting, and was travelling towards Port Isaac.' About an hour and a half later, Mrs Borne of Mount Pleasant was looking out over the bay from her garden when she saw what she thought was a half submerged black boat with a man standing on the end. But the most graphic description was given by temporary postman Mr S.J. Honey, who was delivering letters to Miss Edith Donnithorne at Castle Rock when he looked out to sea and exclaimed, 'There's the Loch Ness monster!' 'So it is!' cried Miss Donnithorne, and ran for her field glasses. Mr Honey told a *Western Morning News* reporter: 'I saw a monstrous thing. It had a big head just like a seal's, a goose-like neck, which must have been standing at least 4 feet out of the water, and there was a huge hump on its back resembling a big barrel. Floating behind on the surface of the water was a tremendous tail, tapering to a point. The creature was between 30 and 40 feet in length. From the edge of Castle Rock one could have jumped on its back. It was going along smoothly just like a yacht, heading for Port Gaverne, and unfortunately going away from me. Then it suddenly sank. There was no wash or dive, it just went down flat. I was watching it for quite 5 minutes, and in the beautifully clear light I could see the sun shining on its glossy black body.'

Mr Honey, who was the secretary of Port Isaac British Legion, insisted that he was a teetotaller. 'I have seen all kinds of fish in 40 years at sea,' he declared, 'and I have never seen the like of this monster before. It was no fish, and more resembled a large amphibian. If I had been at the bottom of the cliff nearby, I would have run away. Practically everyone I have told has treated it as a joke, but I swear by it!' Miss Donnithorne thought that the creature was going to strike the rocks, from which the screaming seagulls hastily took flight. 'It was the most frightening thing,' she said. 'I had never seen such a creature before, although I was born at Port Isaac.'

All this created great excitement, and folk were left wondering if it was a second Loch Ness monster, or whether the first one had wandered away from Loch Ness. They rather hoped that Port Isaac was going to have a monster of its own. However, the local fishermen were sceptical about all this. The sea was their domain, and they wanted to see it with their own eyes before believing.

The strange marine monster was seen in the swiftly flowing waters of the River Gannel, Newquay, by several witnesses a month later. Mr R.H. Northey, proprietor of the Fern Pit Tea Gardens at Pentire, was the first to spot it. He was walking down his garden path immediately above the river with his brother-in-law at about 7 o'clock in the evening, and was surprised to see the 25 foot monster gliding up the river on the full spring tide. Having progressed about a quarter of a mile beyond that point, it suddenly submerged in a pool which was thought to be about 16 feet deep. Seven or eight minutes later they saw the huge creature almost beneath the spot where they were standing, speeding towards the open sea. 'The water was disturbed considerably,' Mr Northey told a *Western Morning News* reporter. 'It was at least 25 to 30 feet long. It was black and glossy. Its head, several times bigger than a man's head, was just above the water. On its back was an extremely huge hump, and flowing behind was a long tail. The strange creature resembled an artist's impression of the Loch Ness monster. It was going just like a submarine on top of the water, and its speed was very fast.' He said that there were mullet in the pool, which may have been the reason it submerged. He was very lucky to witness a repeat performance the following evening, in the presence of a visitor, who suggested that it could be captured if a strong net were set out and properly manoeuvred. Fortunately that did not happen, and let us hope that these wonderful creatures, who have managed to evade the negative impact of mankind for so long, never have to be sacrificed to satisfy our curiosity. They inhabited the planet long before our own species existed, and might possibly outlive us.

My brother and I agree that, now, whenever the sea is exceptionally calm, as it was on that July evening in 1985, we half expect to see the engagingly familiar profile of the sea monster, which will seem like an old friend. Definitive proof of this species' existence will surely amount to a scientific breakthrough comparable to the discovery of intelligent life on another planet. But although I should be very pleased to tell the sceptics 'I told you so!' I think there is a lot to be said for the sea retaining some of its secrets.

THE NOTORIOUS
LIGHTFOOT BROTHERS

There was consternation in the little market town of Wadebridge in February 1840 when news got around that there had been a highway robbery, for this sort of thing tended not to happen around these parts. It seems that Mr Derry, a miller from Hingdon Mill, had been on his way home after a busy day at Wadebridge Market, when he dropped into a public house at Egloshayle Churchtown for a glass or two of grog to wet his whistle. He was in buoyant mood, and it became obvious to all there that he had done well at the market that day. If he had been a little more sober, he might have noticed three shifty characters, who had been watching him, slip outside just as he was preparing to leave. He had not gone far along the lane, when three men suddenly leapt out from a hedge and dealt him a blow which knocked him off his horse. Then they rifled his pockets and made off with the seventy or eighty pounds he had made that day. Fortunately for him, the effects of the grog did not allow him to put up any resistance, and this probably saved his life. Great was the alarm when reports of this attack reached other parts of the area, particularly among farmers setting off for Bodmin Market the next day. Many hastily arranged to travel in groups and one man of doughty spirit and determination was said to have provided himself with a couple of pistols, promising to let the daylight into the person of anyone who might venture to attack *him*.

After a good and convivial day's trading, a well-known

Wadebridge merchant, Nevell Norway, set off home from Bodmin on his little grey mare at about 10 pm. The night was moonlit, but slightly overcast. He caught up with a farming acquaintance and they journeyed on together, overtaking another farmer as they went. However, after Mount Charles Gate, Mr Norway found himself on his own.

Sometime later John Hick and Christopher Bowen, who had stayed on in Bodmin, were on their way home when they were hailed by a man in Sladesbridge shouting 'Stop! The horse is gone on before', as if he thought they were trying to catch a horse. Assuming him to be a bit tipsy, they quickened their pace but soon caught sight of a loose horse, which galloped off ahead of them. Feeling uneasy about this, they asked a man they saw near Egloshayle whether he had seen a horse, and he told them that he had noticed a horse that resembled Mr Norway's little mare, which had a saddle, but no rider. They went straight to Mr Norway's house and, not wishing to alarm his wife unnecessarily, asked the waggoner if his master were at home, mentioning the runaway horse. He went to investigate and found that the mare had returned home, and had a bloodstained saddle. The two riders went to get a surgeon, while the anxious waggoner sought help to search for his master.

When Edward Cavell, a servant, and the waggoner reached North Hill, about 2 miles away, they noticed some marks on the road, as if something heavy had been dragged across it. Then by the dim and flickering light of the lantern they made out a bulky shape in a ditch by the roadside. Cavell went to investigate and exclaimed in horror, 'It's poor Master!' Mr Norway was lying on his back in the water with his feet towards the road. He was wearing his greatcoat, which was unbuttoned, and one of his boots was in the stream. They saw evidence of a scuffle and noticed bloodstains at the scene. The two shocked men hoisted the body onto the horse. On their way back to Wadebridge, they ran into Mr Hick and Mr Bowen, who were accompanied by Mr Trehane Tickle, the surgeon. The victim was taken back to his home, where his body was examined by Mr Tickle. He found severe head injuries, inflicted, he surmised, by blows from more than one heavy blunt weapon, which would have caused instant death.

The Lightfoot brothers as they appeared at the bar, James on the left and William on the right. (From an engraving published in the *West Briton*, 1840)

Edward Cavell, who knew his master's habits well, had searched his clothes and found his pocket book, watch and penknife, but an ivory writing tablet, which he always carried with him, was missing, along with his purse and a bunch of keys. He discovered £25 in notes tucked inside his pocket book. When he and the waggoner and others returned to the murder scene later that night, they found two sets of distinctive footprints, the hammer of a gun or pistol and a button from the victim's greatcoat, broken into three pieces. This was discovered 16 feet from the spot where they first noticed blood, suggesting that the scuffle had taken place over that distance. As well as footmarks, there were marks of a bare hand drawn across the ground. Inside a field gate on the opposite side of the road they found his hat, about 15 yards from where it was supposed the body had fallen.

This more brutal version of the earlier crime was committed on Saturday, 8th February. When it was reported to the coroner, Joseph Hamley, the following morning, he travelled from Bodmin to hold an inquest at the Ship Inn in Wadebridge that afternoon.

Having heard the evidence thus far, he ordered the public to withdraw, and told the jury that he thought it appropriate to leave the investigations to the magistrates. They delivered a verdict of wilful murder by person or persons unknown.

Nevell Norway had been held in very high regard by the local community, and over 3,000 people joined the subsequent funeral procession, headed by his family and influential members of society. All the shops in Wadebridge closed for the day. Subscriptions were set up to defray the expenses incurred in the search for the villain and for the welfare of the bereaved family.

Placards offering a reward of £100 for the apprehension of the murderer or murderers attracted a lot of attention, and some folk got carried away in their enthusiasm to claim the reward. The constables had their work cut out following up leads, and the magistrates who assembled daily at the Molesworth Arms were besieged with people making accusations; inevitably, a number of innocent individuals got caught up in all the hysteria. However, during the late evening on 8th February, John Harris, a shoemaker from St Miniver, had passed along the narrow, lonely lane later travelled by Nevell Norway and had noticed two dubious characters loitering near the spot where the murder was committed. Both were of short stature, but one was taller than the other. One was wearing a dark jacket, the other a smock, and both wore hats.

Amongst those apprehended on suspicion was James Lightfoot, a 23 year old labourer from the nearby hamlet of Burlawn. His 36 year old brother William's nervous reaction to the arrest aroused suspicion, which later led to his own arrest. When he was taken before the magistrates, he panicked and made a full confession of his guilt. There was to be no code of honour with this brotherhood of villains, for by betraying James, William thought that he would save his own skin and carry off the reward. However, when they appeared before the magistrates at the Molesworth Arms, they did not look or behave like individuals capable of such a terrible crime. They were both small men, William being the taller and slimmer of the two. James smiled, while William looked nonchalantly around to see if there were any familiar faces amongst the packed assembly.

A witness, Richard Caddy, described how he had been at William's house on the night of the murder, when William arrived home wearing a darkish jacket and trousers that were soaking wet up to his knees. After speaking quietly with his wife in a back room for a few minutes, he emerged, muttered something about having fallen by a well in Selly's Wood, and then disappeared hastily upstairs to bed.

Richard Ayres and his wife Elizabeth, who lived next door to James Lightfoot's family but were not on speaking terms with them, said that they had gone to bed at about 10 o'clock on the night the murder was committed, but had been awoken by a disturbance next door in the early hours of the morning. Mrs Lightfoot was crying, and her husband tried to quieten her, saying, 'Lie still, damn thee, or folks will hear you.' She had retorted that she would not lie still and didn't care if they did hear her. Elizabeth's mother, Betty Bray, who lived with them, reported this.

When Caddy visited James's house on the Sunday morning he noticed a very distinctive horse pistol on the chimney piece. It had a great deal of brasswork and three notches on the barrel, but the lock was missing. Lightfoot said something about breaking a screw when he shot a cat, but would not be drawn on what had become of the lock.

William Vercoe had noticed that fellow labourer William Lightfoot had turned up very early for work the morning after his brother had been held on suspicion and remarked on it. But William said, 'I shan't stop to work – James is taken up.' He then confided, 'There would be nothing known about we, if it had not been for Betty Bray's family hearing James walking in.' Next day he told Vercoe, 'James shot the cat on Wednesday, and the pistol was bloody; and what he has done with it I do not know. People have been talking about us. Whatever is done by James, it is Betty Bray's family that does it. If James is punished, I must be, too.' When Grace Vercoe, William's mother, went to Burlawn, she saw people making a search for the missing parts of the pistol, and William Lightfoot standing by the cottage. So she said to him, 'Well, Jemmy is put to Bodmin. If you are free, Jemmy is free; if he is guilty, you are guilty. Do, Willy, go and confess.' He made no reply. Then she took him to one side and urged him to tell her about the pistol, but he pretended that he did not know what she was talking about. Grace Vercoe rebuked him: 'You know what you have done. If you don't confess, I shall tell what you told my son. If I were you I would confess, and probably you may have the reward. But if it do go bad with you, perhaps your children will have it.' Then she went to the constable's house, and left a message with his wife, telling him to have William taken up. During the course of journeys between Wadebridge and Bodmin gaol, the brothers were put under pressure to make confessions, and the carriage was halted at the murder scene, where they pointed out where Mr Norway's keys and personal papers had been discarded. His purse had been hidden elsewhere, then later thrown in the stream.

The Lightfoot brothers, who were keen to blame each other for the murder of Mr Norway, never exchanged a glance during the hearing before the magistrates. James remained impassive, and William maintained his deadpan demeanour. The prisoners were committed for trial. The crowd jeered as the handcuffed brothers were placed in a fast horse-drawn vehicle and whisked to Bodmin gaol. Feelings were running very high, for the much respected Norways had always been kind to the Lightfoot family, providing them with employment and helping out in times of need. Yet there had been no expression of remorse from either of them. These sons of the sexton of St Breock, who had had the advantage of some schooling in Wadebridge, had long been regarded as idle fellows, who would rather poach than work for an honest living. Their criminal exploits, ranging from stealing poultry, donkey rustling, house breaking and increasingly serious offences, had extended over the county border into Devon. It was thought that several failed attempts at highway robbery had induced them to murder their next victim, to ensure that they got the money.

When the case opened at the Cornwall Lent Assizes in Bodmin, the javelin men, the judge's escort, had difficulty in trying to control the hundreds of people who had travelled from all over the county, hoping to gain entry to the court. They endeavoured to clear a passage for privileged folk, shoving others back and belabouring them over the head with the javelins. The judge took his seat, and the prisoners were brought in and placed at the bar,

An engraving of the murder scene, as it appeared in the *West Briton*.

both appearing cool and self possessed. They were charged with the wilful murder of Nevell Norway on 8th February in the parish of Egloshayle, by striking and beating him on the head with a pistol and stick, inflicting mortal wounds bringing about instant death; they both pleaded 'Not guilty'.

The prisoners did not have counsel acting on their behalf, but they were free to ask questions of the witnesses. Mr Cockburn for the prosecution addressed the jury, pointing out the serious nature of the charge. He outlined the evidence to be put before them; apart from the confessions, he said that the knowledge of the whereabouts of the stolen property was proof of guilt. Both prisoners admitted that they were present at the murder, but each blamed the other for having taken the more prominent part in it.

William and James took the opportunity to question and contradict the witnesses on several occasions, despite the daunting situation. When labourer William Roche stated that he had seen William at about 4 o'clock in Bodmin Market, just as Mr Norway was taking out his purse and handing money over to some gentlemen, William protested that this was not true. And William Vercoe's evidence caused him to say, 'Almost all he has said is false, and I would sooner be hung right up than hear these things said.' Charles Jackson, a London policeman who had been sent down to investigate the murder, described how he had gone to James Lightfoot's house and found part of the horse pistol. While escorting James from Bodmin to Wadebridge he had questioned him, but the judge intervened saying, 'You had no business to question or cross question a man when a magistrate has committed him, and he is being brought up for re-examination'. Nevertheless, the court had heard what was said.

In his confession, James had stated that his brother William knew that Mr Norway would be returning from Bodmin Market with a large sum of money. The brothers had lain in wait by the gate in the narrow lane near the house, and when they heard him coming they emerged, with William to the fore. William told Mr Norway that he had something for him, and when he pulled up his horse his brother struck him on the head with a stick. He held the reins while William knocked him off. After murdering him, William drew the body across the road to the stream, and then they headed off home across the fields.

Richard Harry, a shoemaker to whom James owed money, solved the mystery of the missing writing tablet. For when he went to remove a heavy dresser from his house in lieu of payment, he came upon it underneath. At the end of the case the judge asked William and James if they had anything to say, and both declared, 'I never murdered Mr Norway.'

In summing up the evidence, the judge pointed out that a large reward had been offered, which sometimes helped to track down criminals, but could also tempt people to exaggerate or pervert evidence, and that the jury should bear this in mind when assessing it. If the jury saw any reasonable doubt with regard to the evidence they had heard, the prisoners were entitled to the benefit of the doubt.

It took the jury two minutes to deliver its verdict of 'Guilty', against both prisoners, and this was greeted by a buzz of satisfaction by the public. The judge, who appeared to feel most deeply the painful duty imposed upon him, passed the sentence that they both be taken back to the prison, and then to the place of execution, where they each be hanged by the neck until dead. Their bodies should then be taken down and buried within the precincts of the prison. Whereupon James leaned over the desk and asked if he could tell the court how he had been drawn into the situation by his brother, and William asked for some refreshment, as he had been kept without all day. Both then left the dock, walking as firmly as they had done when entering it.

The condemned prisoners remained cool and nonchalant, eating, drinking and sleeping as if there were nothing pressing upon their minds, and remaining unemotional as their relatives came to see them, and departed. William eventually admitted that when the thieves who had robbed Mr Derry on 7th February got away with it, he and his brother decided to try the same thing. He had been a heavy drinker, gambler and poacher, and put his troubles down to bad company, and failing to observe the Sabbath. He acknowledged that he habitually told lies, and had continued to tell lies, even to the chaplain while in prison. James, who had done a variety of odd jobs around the area, sometimes living-in, had experienced set backs on account of ill health. He was also a heavy drinker and indulged in binges for days on end, but when he got married he turned from drinking to petty crime. He claimed that some unnamed third party had suggested a means of enriching themselves without working, which led to him and his brother planning crimes of a 'heinous nature'. He admitted that he had snapped the pistol twice at 'poor Mr Norway', and that when it failed to fire, his brother struck the first blow with a stick. He had followed this up with the butt end of the pistol, and assisted in dragging the body across the road into the stream. William said that he had hidden the money under a cabbage in the garden, then transferred it to a hole when James was apprehended. He gave James half a sovereign after the murder, and he gave his wife half a sovereign and half-a-crown. She had paid the half crown into the Egloshayle Penny Club with the view of having 7s 6d for next Christmas. When the chaplain sought further explanations on the eve of the execution, William said, 'There will be time enough tomorrow.' But the confessions never came, and so these secrets went with him to his prison grave.

The chaplain preached a sermon in the chapel on the day before their execution, during which he called on the other prisoners to pray for the Lightfoots, who would be dead in 24 hours, pointing out that there was still hope for them in heaven if they truly repented. Most of the prisoners were moved by this, but the brothers showed no emotion. Yet the gaolers heard William urging James to pray that night, and the turnkey found them both on their knees at dawn.

All roads to Bodmin were clogged with travellers, the public houses were overflowing with people, and the price of food and beer rose dramatically. There was something of a carnival atmosphere, with lurid entertainment, and the state of excitement led to fears as to how the mob might behave at the time of the execution. If some authorities considered the spectacle of public hangings to be a deterrent, others saw it as a corrupting influence. Leaflets were distributed, calling on people to preserve order and conduct themselves with decency. The execution was to be carried out in a theatrical setting, with the sheriffs, javelin men and local and special constables occupying an open space below the drop, overlooked by fields large enough to accommodate hundreds of people.

The prospect of being executed that day did not seem to affect the prisoners' appetites at breakfast time. They left final messages for their wives and hoisted up their heavy chains to walk unaided to the chapel for a final service. A solemn procession led by the chaplain made its way towards the scaffold. The brothers shook hands with the dignitaries. The crowd was moved by this, and did not indulge in the usual catcalls, cheers or groans. James started to tremble, but he took his strength from William. When William had the rope around his neck and the cap over his eyes, he called out, 'James, be sure to pray!' The chaplain prayed as the signal was given to the executioner. The bodies were left hanging for an hour before being cut down and placed in black coffins. They were buried in the coalyard just in front of the prison.

At the time of the murder, Nevell Norway's brother Edward,

who was captain of a merchant ship sailing from Manilla to Cadiz, had a terrible dream, which he wrote down shortly after he awoke. In the dream he saw two men attack his brother near a house on the Wadebridge road. One caught the horse by the bridle and snapped a pistol twice, which did not go off. They struck him several blows, knocking him off his horse and killing him, then dragged him across the road and left him there. When Captain Norway mentioned this to his Second Officer, he made light of it, and teased him about West Country folk being so superstitious.

(Note: Nevell Norway was the forebear of Arthur Norway, Cornish historian and author of *Highways and Byways of Cornwall*, and of the novelist Nevil Shute Norway.)

WITCHCRAFT IN CORNWALL

From Ghoulies and Ghosties
And long leggetty beasties
And things that go bump in the night,
Good Lord deliver us!
(Cornish Litany)

The life and culture of Cornwall stems from the landscape. The grandeur of its wild and rugged coastline, the weird and wonderful rock formations of the granite uplands, and the heavenly aura of the southern river valleys undoubtedly influenced the lives and values of those who went before us. Our early ancestors possessed a spirituality and an affinity with the natural world, now lost to us. The wonder of creation and the mystery of how it all came about would have been of paramount importance. Our ancestors recognised forces far beyond the sphere of mankind in nature and in the rhythm of life. Like other tribes throughout the world they probably worshipped the sun and the moon as life giving forces, and attributed supernatural powers to the spirits of the trees, the hills, the springs and other features of the landscape. Clues to their mortal and mystical activities remain in the more enduring granite moorland areas, in the form of ancient settlements, field systems, burial mounds and intriguing standing stones. The positioning of some of these stones demonstrates a remarkably sophisticated knowledge of astronomy and mathematics, and an astronomical clock has been identified on Bodmin Moor. Some of the stones are thought to be waymarkers along the course of

This striking silhouette is on the door of the Museum of Witchcraft in Boscastle.

prehistoric highways, and some with capstones are thought to be eroded burial chambers, while stone circles such as The Hurlers near Minions, The Merry Maidens at Boleigh and the mysterious King Arthur's Hall near St Breward, appear to have been of sacred significance. While geologists and archaeologists may seek scientific explanations for weird, natural or implanted features in the landscape, poets, dreamers and disciples of other-worldliness make of it what they will. There are those who associate the mysterious standing stones with sacrifices, where singing, chanting and all sorts of rituals were carried out.

If our pagan ancestors drew their inspiration from the natural features of the landscape and the impact of the Atlantic elements, following generations have absorbed their human imprints on the landscape in a culture heavy with legend, folklore and superstition. There were forces for good and ill, and as time went by Cornwall became a whimsical dreamland of stone throwing giants, piskies, fairies, mermaids, knockers and demons, and a variety of 'Little People' with a penchant for playing tricks on innocent folk, unless they were appeased.

The traditional occupations of mining and fishing, with their inherent daily dangers, were steeped in superstition, calling for protective rituals. Sprites known as buccas or knockers embodying the spirits of dead miners would keep watch beneath the surface. Those who worked on the land observed ancient customs to keep the Devil at bay, and when things went wrong country folk attributed this to being ill-wished by someone, usually some unfortunate old woman suspected of being a witch. The only way to remove such a curse was to employ a witch or pellar (her male counterpart), whose services were in great demand.

According to some traditions, witches inherited their special skills from the priestesses serving a goddess of long ago, whose powers were usurped by new male-dominated religions, forcing their activities underground. Witches, who were thought to be in league with the Devil, were persecuted throughout Europe. In the Middle Ages any old crone suspected of being a witch might be tortured and burnt at the stake.

Nevertheless, things continued much as before in the rural areas of remote Cornwall. Those who supported witchcraft drew a distinction between the 'black' or evil witches, who were hated and feared, and the benign 'white' witches or wise women, with their special ability to help and heal people. Their activities were inhibited by the forceful Wesleyan influence of the late 18th century, and they were condemned by various Cornish clergymen in the 19th century. However, things continued much as before, with an assortment of witches, wise women and pellars, wizards, charmers, gipsies and fortune tellers offering their services at rural fairs and travelling round the countryside. The witches did not wear conical hats or transport themselves on broomsticks, although it was not unknown for them to take gullible folk for a ride on occasion. Some of the remedies proved remarkably effective and country folk had great faith in these characters. When illness or misfortune struck them or their farm stock, they assumed this to be the result of ill-wishing and summoned those who had the ability to revoke evil spells or achieve cures by supernatural means. Paradoxically, they also lived in fear of being ill-wished by the very people they sought to help them, and so they made regular visits to them, as a sort of insurance policy and to keep them happy. To tide them over between such visits, country dwellers wore a variety of lucky charms to avert the evil eye, and their magical powers were recharged on the next visit to the wise woman or pellar. The charms might be folded in paper bearing the words, 'By the help of the Lord, these will do thee good', and enclosed in a little bag to be worn on the chest. Thus Christianity had become absorbed into the folklore and culture. Indeed, there was a legend associated with St Just in Roseland, about the boy Jesus going there with his tin-trading uncle Joseph of Arimathea. Some subscribe to the theory that the study and practice of the magical arts were learned from the early Celtic saints, who reputedly reached these shores from Wales and Ireland in miraculous style aboard millstones.

In the days when it was believed that spirits freely roamed the Cornish countryside, certain parsons gained a reputation for exorcising restless ghosts, and used their powers to gain a hold over their flock. In West Penwith some notable families impressed the local population with their ability to produce horoscopes, distil strange and magical concoctions, predict the future and lay troublesome spirits to rest. They were held in awe by their humbler neighbours, and being credited with the gift of detecting wrongdoers, they proved to be very effective at keeping troublesome folk in their place. As time went by, others caught on to the idea, and the powerful mantle fell on lowlier shoulders, until virtually every town and village had its own representative of the magical arts, exerting a tremendous influence over the everyday life of the community. If one were not fortunate enough to be the seventh daughter of a seventh daughter, or the seventh son of a seventh son, there were other ways of acquiring the specialist powers. Touching a logan (rocking) stone nine times at midnight might turn a woman into a witch, or it might not. A more reliable method centred on the Giant's Rock near Zennor, in West Penwith. Would-be witches would try to mount the rock nine times without shaking it. However, this was more of a challenge than it seemed, as it was formerly a very sensitive rocking stone, and the task was well nigh impossible. True witches were credited with the ability to take on the form of an animal, and black cats and white hares were particularly significant.

Witches and wizards were thought to have been especially powerful on St George's Eve, April 22nd, and the days after Christmas leading up to Twelfth Night. According to ancient tradition the May Day festivities with music and dancing were designed to scare away evil spirits. The placing of greenery before the doors of dwellings encouraged the spirits of the trees to bestow their blessings on the inhabitants. To prevent or undo witchcraft, the following formula was efficacious, if written on paper and not revealed to any mortal:

R O T A S
O P E R A
T E N E T
A R E P O
S A T O R

If someone felt that they had been bewitched, they might scratch the face of the culprit and draw blood. One poor lady called Jenny Harris, who had the misfortune to be impoverished, getting on in

The mystical Men-an-Tol on the Penwith Moors where pagan rites are still practised today.

years, and embittered by life's experiences, was suspected of being responsible for the evils which befell cattle and the local population. On one occasion a robust, rough and ready washerwoman,who thought she was under the spell of the aged crone, set about her until she drew blood from her badly mutilated arm. This violent assault led to an appearance before the magistrate, who fined the assailant £5. In May 1840 Newlyners carried out a ceremony to dispel the supposed influence of witchcraft from one of the mackerel boats, which had been particularly unsuccessful in netting fish that season. In order to counteract the effects of the spell, part of the fishing gear was burnt, amid the shouts and cheers of those assembled on the shore. A few years later there was some puzzlement about a fishing boat of Padstow that was not having much luck, while the rest of the fleet was enjoying a very plentiful season. Someone suggested that the vessel had been bewitched and it was decided to break the charm by nailing a horseshoe to its timbers; the following night 1,400 fish were caught, convincing everyone that it had been ill-wished. If some people scoffed about belief in the supernatural, most followed the procedures – just in case.

The Redruth area was particularly famous for its witches and wizards, and one wise woman, called Bella, plied a lucrative trade for over 20 years, even though some folk noticed a remarkable similarity about her predictions made at a time when most of the young miners were forced to seek work overseas and usually married before they went. She repeatedly prophesied that they would marry, go abroad to seek their fortunes, and then return and live happily ever after. She modestly told everyone that her fame had spread to 'London church town'. But when a wealthy client from the metropolis called to see her on a Sunday, the ancient witch steadfastly refused a consultation and the 'gain of money', because she would not 'break the Sabbath'.

Another wise woman of the West enjoyed a clientele from all walks of life. She usually charged 'three an' a tanner' for consultations, but had been known to accept small quantities of tea, flour, bacon or other goods in kind, from the impecunious. As an experienced practitioner in her seventies, she was besieged by visitors, who were usually supplied with dried herbs or salt, tied up in small cotton bags. These charms, if worn continuously on the chest, would protect the wearer from bewitchment, the evil eye, bad legs, sore throats and a number of other ills.

One witch, and her clients, gained remarkable benefits from a kennal (polished) stone, which, when passed across the eyes, cured all complaints, present or future. One wizard was renowned for his poultices, which were remarkably efficacious for inflammation and 'joint racking rheums', but when it came to toothache, warts and chilblains, he resorted to charms. Warts could also be cured by rubbing a piece of stolen beef across them, which then had to be buried. The warts withered away as the beef decayed. Alternatively, they might be touched with a pebble, which was then put in a bag and thrown away. However, any finder imprudent enough to open the bag might catch the warts.

Tamsin Blight or Tammy Blee of Helston was one of the county's most renowned white witches, and she was married to a man who claimed similar occult powers. She effected some remarkable cures during her lifetime, and shortly before her death, when she was confined to bed. Some who were brought to her on stretchers were known to have miraculously recovered their health and were able to get up and walk down the stairs unaided.

One of the most mysterious of the wise women lived in an isolated little cottage in the wild and rocky landscape near Zennor. She had tame sheep, goats, black cats, dogs, white hares and poultry, which used to follow her about wherever she went. She never ventured very far, although she may have joined the other witches who assembled at Trewey at midnight on Midsummer Eve. Those who arrived at her door in need of healing might be given charms, salves, potions, ointments or magical water of her own distilling. Her speciality was identifying ill-wishers and releasing the victims by inflicting pain on waxen effigies of the culprits. She had knowledge of the black arts, and would threaten to forsake white witchery for black if provoked. The old dame, known as An' Maggey, or Margaret the Witch, belonged to a once proud family from Morvah, who were related to other leading families of the area. They had disowned her for marrying a handsome young sailor, who was later drowned at sea. Two or three times a year the old crone would don her youthful finery and dream of happier days. Most of the time she would sit at her spinning wheel, surrounded by the exotic souvenirs from far-away places that were given to her by her lover of long ago.

Anyone who thinks that the culture of witches and witchcraft is confined to history is very much mistaken. The ancient arts never really disappeared, and there are a growing number of witches and covens interpreting the mystical pagan rites and rituals in their own way, particularly amid the ancient granite landscape of West Penwith.

A MOORLAND MURDER

Agrim granite monument beside a moorland stream at the foot of Roughtor recalls a notorious 19th century tragedy which excited the Victorians and has been the focus of morbid curiosity ever since. It stands on a plinth with a rough hewn base, and bears the inscription: 'THIS MONUMENT was ERECTED by PUBLIC SUBSCRIPTION in MEMORY of CHARLOTTE DYMOND who was MURDERED here by MATTHEW WEEKES on SUNDAY April 14 1844'. Generations of moorlanders and a few level-headed service personnel from nearby tented encampments have claimed that the young servant girl's restless spirit haunts this wild and eerie place.

Charlotte did not have the best start in life, having been born out of wedlock to a young Boscastle woman who always resented her. When she was about 10 years old she was packed off to the northern fringes of Bodmin Moor to work in service at Penhale Farm which was run by a kindly widow called Phillipa Peter. Charlotte had grown into a comely young woman, and tried to make the most of her lot, hoping, no doubt, to do better in life than her mother. She took a pride in her appearance, wearing pretty clothes fashioned from fabrics acquired at local fairs by a local dressmaker, along with an array of scarves, beads and other stylish accessories. Although rather shy, she liked the lads to notice her, and could be a bit of a flirt at times.

Young Charlotte had first met Matthew Weekes when they were both taken on by Mrs Peter in 1838. However, she took another position at Tremail about three years later, and it was while she was there that she started keeping company with Matthew, who was six years her senior. Although not the most handsome and dashing of suitors, with his pock-marked face, missing front teeth and slightly limping gait, he was steady, prudent with money, and had good husband potential for a girl in her position. He was also clothes conscious, and looked a cut above the usual farm labourer when turned out in his natty outfits, with velvet jackets, smart ties and fancy waistcoats.

Matthew did not find it easy to attract the girls, and was pleased when Mrs Peter took Charlotte back into her employment. Their relationship had been well established; he kept her best clothes in his bedroom box in the room he shared with Mrs Peter's son John, a fellow employee called John Stevens and a young farm lad; Charlotte in turn did some of his washing and ironing. Everything was on an even keel as far as Matthew was concerned, until Thomas Prout, an old adversary, who had previously lived and worked with Matthew, suddenly turned up, having found work in the vicinity. They had a terrible row, during which Prout said that he had a mind to take up with Charlotte. Matthew lost his temper and called his rival a few choice names.

If this desirable young lady fancied she had found happiness at last, she got a shock as Lady Day approached, when Mrs Peter gave her notice to quit. This quarter day (25th March), like Michaelmas, was the traditional time for farmers to take on or lay off workers. In the event Charlotte remained at Penhale beyond the date she had been expected to leave.

All seemed well on that fateful Sunday morning in April, when Matthew was in a lighthearted mood, seen by Mrs Peter to be teasing Charlotte by flourishing a letter before her and holding it beyond her reach. But frivolity gave way to anger and jealousy when he noticed Thomas Prout in conversation with Charlotte in the courtyard at about 11 am. He rushed into the house in agitation, asked Mrs Peter what they could be talking about, then rushed out again. At about 4.15 on that rainy, murky afternoon Charlotte came downstairs decked out in all her finery followed by Matthew, who went outside after her. Charlotte returned to the porch to slip pattens (overshoes with wooden platforms poised over an oval metal framework) on over her shoes to save them being spoilt in the wet mud. As she was about to leave Mrs Peter called her back to ask where she was going at that time of day, for it was too late for the afternoon service in the chapel and too early for the evening one. She was none the wiser when Charlotte merely said that she would not be back in time to do her share of the milking, but that Matthew would, and would stand in for her. She had been evasive because she had agreed to meet Thomas Prout at Tremail chapel and did not want Matthew to know about it.

Charlotte and Matthew seemed quite well matched as they set off up the muddy lane in their Sunday best. She was sporting her new Easter bonnet trimmed with ribbons, and wore a red shawl over a full length green striped gown. Her white cotton gloves were immaculate and she carried a black silk bag trimmed with lace. Matthew was wearing a dark velvet frock coat, his best boots, well pressed trousers, and carried an umbrella to shield them both from the rain.

Mrs Peter was in the kitchen with her son and John Stevens when Matthew arrived home well past milking time, at 9.30 pm, and she asked him where Charlotte was. He mumbled that he did not know, as he often did after they had been out together; she usually turned up a few minutes later. Mrs Peter said he should have brought her straight in, as it was past supper time. Being bombarded with questions as to what had been going on, Matthew gave them to understand that he went only a short distance with Charlotte, and thought she had gone off with Tom Prout.

The three men retired to bed an hour later, Matthew pausing to take off his best boots at the foot of the stairs, where they remained all night. Mrs Peter stayed up until 11.30 pm, waiting for Charlotte, and the next morning called to Matthew to come down and help with the milking, as Charlotte had not returned. In the daylight she could see that his boots were very muddy, and when she went up to his room later in the day she found that the feet and legs of his stockings left at his bedside were caked with mud right up to the garters. She told him it looked as if he had been out on the moors cutting peat, but he insisted that the roads had been very muddy.

Mrs Peter was very worried, and continued to question Matthew over the next few days. When pressed Matthew said that

The Charlotte Dymond memorial on Bodmin Moor.

he had accompanied Charlotte as far as Higher Down Gate, and thought she had gone out on the moors, while he had gone in the opposite direction to 'All Drunkard' (the local name for Hallworthy), to call on the Westlake family (who were related to Mrs Peter). He claimed that they had all been out, apart from the widow Sally Westlake. Pressed still further on Charlotte's whereabouts, he declared, 'If I must tell you the truth, she has gone to Blisland into service, for Mrs Langston has got her an easier place than yours!' When he blamed Mrs Peter for having given her notice to quit she countered by alleging that it was his jealousy that had driven the poor maid away and that there were plenty of young men in Blisland to make a fuss of her. But, still worried about Charlotte's well-being, Mrs Peter pointed out that Blisland was a ten-mile walk across the wild moors, and she would never have got there by nightfall after setting out so late in the day. Matthew was reassuring – Charlotte would have stopped over at Cain Spears's place at Brown Willy, and gone on the next day; the letter with which he had been teasing her was from Mrs Peter's niece in Blisland, inviting her to come and work there.

As the week went on local folk kept questioning Matthew about Charlotte's disappearance, and some suggested that he had 'put her out on the moors' so that Tom Prout could not have her. Mrs Peter tackled him about these rumours after supper on the Saturday night following Charlotte's disappearance, adding 'Matthew, I am quite frightened. If you have hurted the girl, you ought to be hung in chains.' He made no comment, and ignored her calls as he went upstairs to bed. On the Sunday morning, as he was outside tending the bullocks, Mrs Peter asked her son and John Stevens to go across the moor to check the situation at Brown Willy and Blisland. Matthew saw them head off in the direction of Higher Down Gate, and realised where they were going. He went upstairs and changed into his best clothes, prompting Mrs Peter to comment about the light coloured trousers he had worn the previous week being spattered with mud right up the front. She also thought it odd that he was carrying his umbrella on this sunny Sunday as he left the house. He would not be drawn on where he was going, but gave her to understand he would be back in time for dinner.

Mrs Peter was beginning to think that Matthew has done a

bunk when her daughter Mary Westlake came to see her later that day. It soon became apparent that Matthew had not called to see the various branches of the Westlake family on the previous Sunday as he had claimed. This being the case, the two women decided to go through some of his things, and discovered one of Charlotte's handkerchiefs in the pocket of the dark velvet jacket he had worn on that day, and a badly ripped shirt which had been clumsily mended with dark thread. Matthew had still not returned at nightfall, when John Peter and John Stevens arrived home with the news that neither Cain Spears nor the Langstons had any knowledge of Charlotte's lonely trudge across the moor, and that Rebecca Langston had never promised her a job nor written her a letter . . .

A 12-strong search party including John Peter and John Stevens set out across the wild and desolate moor on Tuesday morning (nine days after Charlotte went missing). After making their way to Higher Down Gate, they headed southwards to an area in which a local farmer had seen a couple walking in the rain with an umbrella on that Sunday, and fancied that he had recognised Matthew by his familiar twisting gait. Another farmer out on horseback had also reported seeing a man and woman behaving strangely at that time; walking together, separating and coming face-to-face, with the woman repeatedly turning her back on the man. He had asked them if they were lost or if anything were amiss, but had received no reply. As far as the searchers were concerned, it seemed like looking for a needle in a very large haystack. However, one sharp-eyed observer noticed some regular oval disturbances in the wet turf near the isolated Lan Lavery Rock, which they identified as the distinctive imprint made by ladies' pattens. They followed these tracks down to a lonely and desolate area near Roughtor Ford, where the party divided to examine the treacherous marshland.

Later that day one of the searchers came upon the body of young Charlotte Dymond, lying on her back in the water ruts by a stream, with her throat cut from ear to ear. His urgent calls brought the rest of the party rushing to the scene. Most of them knew the victim well, and were sickened by the horrifying spectacle. Her head and trunk had been partially in the water, and she was surrounded by diluted blood which had oozed out from the jagged wound in her neck. One of her arms was stretched out above her shoulder, and the other was down by her side; one knee was bent up, while the other was almost straight. Part of her upper clothing had been ripped away, and her crumpled gown was pulled up above her knees, leaving part of her stomach exposed; one stocking was half way down her leg, while the other remained in place, secured by a garter. Beads from her precious coral necklace were strewn above her head, and these were carefully retrieved. There was no indication of there having been a scuffle in this vicinity, and no murder weapon was found. A surgeon was summoned to examine the body, before it was placed on a cart, trundled across the rough moorland terrain and deposited in an outhouse of Penhale Farm. After carrying out a more detailed examination, the surgeon came to the conclusion that the young woman's death was caused by an extensive wound to the neck, inflicted with considerable force by a rather blunt knife or cutting instrument. It could have been self-inflicted, but that was unlikely. He saw no sign of any sexual assault, and she was not pregnant. In the meantime a search was going on for Charlotte's red shawl, neckerchief, bonnet, bonnet cap, shoes, pattens, gloves and black silk handbag, and most of these were found concealed under moss in a bloodstained turf-pit, about half a mile from where the body was found. However, it remained a mystery as to what had become of her gloves and handbag. Further investigations by local policemen yielded some rather muddled evidence about suspicious footprints found in the area and attributed to Matthew's boots.

After making his hurried departure from Penhale on Sunday, 21st April, Matthew had called to see some old friends at Coad's Green, near North Hill, arriving there at about 3 pm. They noticed that he was rather preoccupied and ill-at-ease, and made no response when asked how Charlotte was. When their young daughter proudly told him that she had a handbag of her own, he said that he had a bag belonging to a young woman, and produced from his breast pocket a black silk bag trimmed with lace, then replaced it. He departed at 9 pm, explaining that he would be staying overnight with his mother, and returning to Penhale early next morning.

The courtroom at Shire Hall, Bodmin, where Matthew Weekes was tried. (Taken with kind permission of 'The Courtroom Experience', Shire Hall, Bodmin.)

By this time the hunt was on for the fugitive, and Constable John Bennett of South Petherwin, who knew that Matthew had relatives in Plymouth, found him on the Hoe next day in the company of his sister and brother-in-law. He greeted him by saying, 'Matthew, how are you?' To which the wanted man replied, 'Pretty well.' 'You must go with me,' said the Constable. 'Where?' said Matthew. 'I must take you before Mr John King Lethbridge.' 'What for?' asked Matthew innocently. 'You know what for!' retorted the Constable, and tried to find a gentle way of breaking the shocking news to the brother-in-law and heavily pregnant sister.

Matthew was taken into custody, when the missing gloves and bag were discovered in his jacket and waistcoat pockets. Once across the Cornish border, he was interrogated by several constables and charged with the murder of Charlotte Dymond. He gave them to understand that he had not been keeping company with Charlotte since Lady Day, 'but some other chaps had.' He was taken on to Camelford for further investigations, and appeared before a magistrate known to one and all as 'King John' in the parlour of the All Drunkard Inn at Hallworthy. The magistrate found it a case of *prima facie* murder and committed him to Bodmin Gaol to await trial.

After an autopsy and inquest, various people had come forward to give evidence about distant sightings on the moor that murky Sunday evening, which did not always align with details of the ill-fated couple, and some of the witnesses at the trial which followed came up with additional evidence against the prisoner, sometimes conflicting with what they had said at a previous hearing. The circumstantial evidence weighed very heavily against Matthew, whose alibi was discredited, although certain significant factors were overlooked – he was not the only person out on the moor that day, and there was the possibility of suicide. But in fact Matthew Weekes was deemed to be a murderer before being questioned, and even before the body was found.

Three hymns, specially written for the harrowing occasion, were sung on the way to poor Charlotte's funeral, and she was buried in an unmarked grave in the churchyard at Davidstow. This moving, real-life sequence of events, reminiscent of a Victorian novel in its tragi-romanticism, captured the imagination of an eager public, who saw it as a classic case of a spurned lover murdering his sweetheart rather than facing the prospect of losing her to another man.

Such notoriety focused more than usual attention on the Temperance Society's annual meeting at the foot of Roughtor that June (two months after the murder, and six weeks before the trial). This turned out to be something of a jamboree, with thousands of people converging on the area for a variety of sports and pastimes. Earnest speakers seeking to address the rally found themselves in competition with cheapjacks shouting their wares, in an event which found a place in local folklore as the Roughtor Revels. A somewhat incongruous black flag erected on the spot where Charlotte's body was found prompted many people to contribute towards the erection of a memorial, and thus the names of the killer and his victim were carved in granite for posterity.

An excited mob of curious onlookers had observed Matthew being taken to Camelford before being despatched to Bodmin Gaol, looking apparently unconcerned. His characteristic facial expression, where a heavy brow, missing teeth and smallpox scarring combined to give the illusion that he was smirking when his face was in repose, did nothing to help him during the trial which lay ahead. There was a veritable multitude of people and more spectator excitement at the time of the Bodmin Assizes that July, when the learned judges and their smart legal entourage swept in from Exeter in colourful style and with much impressive ceremony before proceedings commenced in the newly built Shire Hall. Although other trials were taking place at the same time, this was the one that everybody had come to see, and there was a mad rush to get inside as the courtroom doors were opened. When this unseemly situation had been sorted out, the very mundane looking individual accused of playing the evil role in this tragic crime of passion was led in, wearing a fancy waistcoat with glass buttons, a blue shooting jacket and grey trousers. The indictment was read out, and he pleaded 'Not guilty'.

Matthew was not able to give his own version of events during the trial, for defendants were not allowed to give evidence in those days. Frederick Slade, the defence lawyer, was concerned that his client would not have a fair trial, on account of all the far ranging press coverage and intensive publicity, with everyone regarding him as guilty before he had been tried.

The courtroom was tense as the foreman of the jury delivered the verdict of 'Guilty', but Matthew seemed composed. He remained impassive as Judge Patterson told him that his time left in the world was short, although he was young, and that as there was no apparent reason for mercy, there was nothing to prevent the law from taking its course. As there was no hope in this world, he urged the condemned man to seek forgiveness from the Almighty in the next. The judge went on to explain to Matthew that he would be taken from there and hung from the neck, and that his body would be buried within the prison precincts. Suddenly the full gravity of the situation hit the young man. He slumped backwards and was carried from the courtroom in a state of unconsciousness by two turnkeys.

Whilst awaiting his execution, Matthew was all too well aware of the disgrace he had brought upon his family, was very contrite, and suffered severely from stress-related sickness. Nevertheless he was said to have conducted himself with dignity. He reportedly made a confession, stressing that the murder was not a premeditated act. Apparently he had followed Charlotte as she left the farm, and joined her for a walk on the moor. Initially the conversation had been about nothing in particular, but things got heated when he mentioned that he had seen her behaving disgracefully with another man. He was so incensed when the woman he loved more than anyone in all the world turned her back on him, retorting that she would do as she liked, and had nothing further to say to him, that he drew out his pocket knife and lunged towards her. He came to his senses and put it away, but lost control when she repeated those fateful words, little realising what was about to happen. Then 'Lord have mercy on me!' she cried, as she toppled backwards with blood cascading from her neck, landing near the stream. He hid her clothes and flung the knife away on the way home.

The day before his execution the illiterate prisoner put his sign to two letters. He bade farewell to his family, sending his love and good wishes, and requesting them to settle his worldly affairs and share out his clothing and other personal effects. He also urged his brothers to adopt a more Christian way of life. The other letter, addressed to Mrs Peter, the mistress of Penhale, who had borne witness against him at the trial, expressed forgiveness, thanked her for her kindness and acknowledged previous advice about the error of his ways. He also thanked the judge and jury who had given him no more than he deserved, and the chaplain for endeavouring to save his soul. Both letters warned young men and maidens against putting too much trust in the opposite sex, for 'See what a wretched end I have come to by loving too true.'

The public execution that August provided the ultimate cautionary, morbid spectacle for the thousands who converged on Bodmin from all directions, on foot and by every available mode of transport. The streets were crammed by 11 o'clock, and by noon an estimated crowd of 20,000 was congregated at viewpoints overlooking the drop. As the prison clock reached the last stroke of twelve, the chapel bell started tolling and the executioner appeared, followed by Matthew and the chaplain. The wretched prisoner was so weak that he could hardly stand, and the executioner was obliged to help and support him as he adjusted the rope and pulled the cap over his face. There was a tense silence as the chaplain read a short prayer, and he and the hangman retreated from the drop. But many screamed and some passed out as the heavy trap fell and the murderer hung lifeless before them.

In the grim and empty anti-climax which followed this sickening spectacle, the subdued multitude dispersed; some headed for home and others shuffled off to the public houses or sought other diversions. The victim's body remained suspended for the customary hour and one minute, and, by the early morning, life was continuing much as usual in the town. However, nobody was ever likely to forget such a macabre experience, where the punishment was generally agreed to have fitted the grisly crime.

THE SILVANUS TREVAIL ENIGMA

Saturday, 7th November 1903 promised to be like any other day on the Great Western Railway, when the smartly uniformed guard waved his flag and the 11.40 up train pulled out of Truro station. If a passenger in a third class compartment thought his newly arrived travelling companion seemed ill-at-ease and looked very gloomy, it was understandable, as he was attired in mourning and obviously on his way to a funeral. Just after the train left Lostwithiel, the man in black got up from his seat and made his way along the corridor. When the train had passed through a small tunnel, several ladies seated in the last compartment of a corridor carriage noticed a stocky and distinguished looking gentleman making his way towards the ladies' lavatory. Mrs Leah May, who occupied a corner seat facing the ladies' lavatory, thought it strange and improper. She put her hand on the handle of the door with the intention of going out and telling him so, but then paused for a brief discussion with her fellow passengers. While they were expressing their indignation, he emerged from the closet, looked back along the corridor and placed his hand on the brass bar of the window to steady himself as the train gave a lurch. But having realised that he was being watched, and perhaps feeling embarrassed, he backed into the lavatory again. As the train slackened speed on the approach to Bodmin Road Station, a sudden shot rang out, and Mrs May shouted 'That gentleman's shot himself!' and she rushed to the lavatory to see what she could do to help him. She found him

Cornish architect Silvanus Trevail, one time President of the Society of British Architects, wearing his presidential medal. (The Royal Cornwall Museum, Truro)

in a stooping position with blood streaming from his head. Various people had heard the sound of a gun, but they, like the gentlemen in the next compartment, tried to shrug off any notion that anything untoward had happened, and her immediate appeal for help fell on deaf ears.

Mrs May called out for assistance as the train reached the station, and Porter Pindar, who had heard the loud report and thought a detonator had exploded, also a doctor and some policemen, who had happened to be on the train, saw the body of the unfortunate man who had apparently committed suicide in the ladies' lavatory. PC Botheras of Mevagissey later stated that the man was practically sitting on his heels, with both hands between his legs. He held a revolver in his right hand, and his finger was still on the trigger. Blood was running from a wound in the middle of his forehead and had spilt all over his hands and the revolver. His face was perspiring and steaming. The revolver had five chambers, one of which had been discharged, and it was assumed that the man had positioned himself in front of the mirror in order to direct the weapon accurately to the centre of his forehead. By now, everyone on the platform and most of the passengers in the train had realised that something was seriously amiss, and they watched in horror as the lifeless body was removed from the train and placed in the waiting room. The station master, who had been promptly alerted to the terrible happening on the train, was astounded to recognise the tragic figure as Mr Silvanus Trevail, the famous architect, who was one of Cornwall's finest sons. The folk of Truro could scarcely credit that this much-respected, high profile man could possibly have committed suicide by shooting himself in a railway carriage. He would have been the very last person they would have expected to do such a thing, and they would not have believed it, had the news not come from trusted railway officials. As the *West Briton* put it, 'That such a strong-minded, iron-willed man as Mr Silvanus Trevail, F.R.I.B.A., should lose his mental balance, and seek self-destruction, was, indeed, a staggerer for most people.'

On hearing of his uncle's death earlier that week, Silvanus had written to his cousin in Luxulyan, sympathising with him and saying that it was his intention to be present at the funeral on Saturday afternoon, 'if not prevented by what I am unable to control.' He added, 'You will, I am sure, be sorry to hear that I am no better.' His assistant, Alfred Cornelius, thought that he had seemed 'thoroughly unhinged' at this time. On the fateful morning he had seen him off in a horse-drawn cab at 11.30 am, attired in black frock coat and silk hat, to catch the 11.40 *Cornishman* express from Truro station. He should have taken a ticket to Bridges, which was the nearest station to Luxulyan on the Newquay line, and changed trains at Par. But in the event he bought a third class ticket to St Austell, settled himself into a corridor compartment occupied by one other person, and failed to alight when the train reached that station.

Although he may have appeared to be in a dark and dismal world of his own, no one would have guessed that their fellow traveller had a revolver secreted about his person and that he was preparing to put his deadly plan into action as the train left Lostwithiel. Had the man whose life was about to be extinguished been symbolically preparing to mourn himself as he dressed in black on that tragic day? What a heartrending situation it was for the other relatives converging on Luxulyan for the family funeral. As Silvanus's sister, Mrs Rundle, and her husband were passing through Lostwithiel in a mourning coach, Mr Rundle was discreetly informed of what had transpired. Although shocked and shaken, he managed to withold the sad news from his wife until after the funeral. The terrible tidings were quietly whispered amongst those gathered outside the church before the service began. They, like everyone else, wondered what had driven the family's most successful son to despair.

The bright lad, born into a family of Luxulyan yeomen farmers on 31st October 1851, had always had an ambition to make his mark in life and displayed an awareness of his surroundings and a flair for drawing and model-making from an early age. As a schoolboy, Silvanus had noticed that the sound made by two cracked bells in his own parish church did not compare favourably with the fine peals he had heard whilst visiting Lanlivery, Lanivet, Fowey, St Winnow and St Austell, and he resolved to do something about it one day. Having attended a local school from 1857 to 1865, he went on to Ledrah House School in St Austell and other educational institutions, subsequently passing his Oxford and Cambridge Junior and Senior examinations with flying colours. He was then apprenticed to a London architect. His return to Cornwall in 1872 was timely, in that it coincided with a need to build new schools as outlined in a recent education act, and his first commission was to design the Elementary Board School at Mount Charles, St Austell. As it was the first school of its kind to be built in Britain, his work was featured in the *Illustrated London News*. Having stolen a march on his professional rivals, he went on to construct 35 new schools across the county over the next eight years in his solid and sober Victorian Gothic style.

Silvanus Trevail had become a Cornish institution with his

readily identifiable scholarly structures, colloquially known as 'Trevail's Landmarks', scattered across the Cornish countryside. He was also stamping his style across the Tamar, in Devon, London and other places far beyond, acting as architect for many public bodies. He designed banks, libraries, hospitals, churches and chapels, as well as prestigious houses, hotels and other commercial premises. His design for the Central Technical School in Truro was featured at the Royal Academy Exhibition of 1898. He was a member of several high-profile organisations in the capital, where his worth as an architect was well recognised. He had become a fellow of the Royal Institution of British Architects at a young age, and he was also an enthusiastic member of the Royal Institution of Cornwall, based on Truro, and was exceptionally well versed in local history. So his interests were very far ranging. These were heady days, and the dynamic extrovert enjoyed all the power, influence and high-profile social interaction that went with success.

Silvanus had taken up residence in Truro around 1880 and soon achieved prominence in the city's affairs. He was elected a member of the town council, became chairman of the finance committee, chief magistrate and mayor. When Cornwall County Council was established in 1889, he represented Truro and was a strong municipal reformer and advocate for the recognition of local government. He was a formidable opponent, who stuck to his point of view and bore grudges against those guilty of perceived injustices.

During the course of his travels on the Continent, Silvanus had noticed how much more advanced hotel accommodation was than in his native Cornwall, which had equally stunning scenery to enchant discerning tourists, with railway systems extending to points along the coast well suited to becoming exclusive tourist resorts. He realised the importance of the railways, but sought to break the stronghold of the Great Western Railway by encouraging their rival, the London and South Western Railway, to make inroads into what they regarded as their territory. Was it a coincidence that he made his spectacular departure from this life aboard a GWR train? The Cornish Hotels Company, founded in 1890, set out to establish a string of first class hotels around the

Silvanus Trevail was confronted by rioters during the building of the Headland Hotel, Newquay. (Taken with kind permission of the Headland Hotel)

coast of Cornwall. The aim was to create dominating clifftop structures, far removed from the masses, where expensive holiday dreams came true. This flurry of hotel building on sensitive sites of exceptional natural beauty was not without its complications, and the original plan to construct King Arthur's Castle Hotel so close to the ruins of the ancient castle at Tintagel caused such a stir that a fund was set up for the purchase of Barras Nose, making it, in 1897, the first coastal site to be acquired by the National Trust. The hotel opened in 1899.

Silvanus had seen the potential of Newquay, with its beautiful scenery, sandy beaches and established rail link, as a resort to rival some of the great watering places on the Continent. His bold plan to purchase a clifftop site for the construction of the Atlantic Hotel was ridiculed by some, who nicknamed it 'Trevail's Folly', but they were to be proved wrong. Having dissociated himself from the

Cornish Hotels Company, he set his sights on building the Headland Hotel, which was to be 'the finest hotel west of Bournemouth'. Never one to shun publicity or demonstrate much tact, he declared that it would be comparable with some of the finest hotels in Europe and America, with the highest standards of building, furnishings and catering, employing the best available staff and attracting first class people to Cornwall. It would be a luxury hotel with lifts and electric lighting, twice the size of the Atlantic and far better appointed. As if he had not said too much already, he fell for a newspaper reporter's loaded question as to whether this would beat the Atlantic's situation by responding provocatively: 'Won't we though! We will get right in front of it, with a far better approach and, being far further westwards and seawards, we will have a finer ocean view. We take in quite as much of the coastline eastwards as they do, and far more to the westwards. We, too, shall have an ocean view from every window and no view of the objectionable parts of the town of Newquay as is the case from the south front of the Atlantic.' By his unguarded remarks, he had run down Newquay and humiliated those associated with the Atlantic Hotel. The famous architect had alienated himself from a lot of people, who did not like his buccaneering style. Was he really as thick skinned as he made out? His actions were making waves. The Atlantic Hotel, worried about such competition, sought to improve their amenities by enclosing part of the headland. This was traditionally regarded as common land and was used for the drying of fishing nets and the enjoyment of the public. Local feelings were running very high and, before the wall was finished, about 400 protesters who had gathered in Commercial Square demolished it stone by stone to loud shouts and cheers. Anyone trying to stop them got some rough treatment. The disorderly conduct lasted for three days, causing extensive damage in the hotel grounds. Silvanus, who had fallen out with his former company was quite confident that nothing like that could happen to *him*.

If he had anticipated plain sailing in regard to the construction of the Headland Hotel, he was in for a nasty shock. No sooner had work begun than a rampaging mob descended on the site, overturning, wrecking and demolishing anything they could lay their hands on, and pushing the wooden site office over the cliff. Silvanus, the chairman of the hotel company, left London when he heard about this. When he arrived at Newquay railway station, he was met by a howling, spitting, angry mob, keen to vent their anger on him, although the project would provide employment for hundreds of local people. The man who had done so much for Newquay braved a noisy, hostile crowd who pelted him with mud, stones, turves, eggs, apples, sawdust and a range of other missiles as he made his way to the site and calmly carried out an inspection. The excited mob became more violent as he returned to the station, and the policemen, who had been there to protect him, were almost knocked off their feet by the surging crowd. They succeeded in pinning Silvanus and his protectors against the station railings, making taunts, and threatening to maul him. The architect apparently took all this in his stride, but the stress must have been building up for this energetic and enterprising man, whose capacity for work was phenomenal.

The controversy over building hotels on conspicuous coastal sites made Silvanus the target of criticism from farmers and fishermen defending their traditional rights, and also from the new breed of middle class settlers from up country and preservationists, who feared that any land commanding a beautiful view was vulnerable to developers. As it transpired, his work served to promote tourism – and the conservation movement.

Silvanus had never married. He took an emotional battering in 1902, when he lost his mother, and then his father, to whom he had been particularly close. His parents were buried in the churchyard at Luxulyan, where many generations of Trevails already rested. Silvanus erected a fine Celtic cross and took the opportunity to present the long envisaged peal of six bells to the church in their memory. At this time he was engaged on an extension project at the County Asylum in Bodmin. Apart from his numerous duties as an architect, he was travelling a lot and had extensive municipal obligations in Truro, as well as his responsibilities as President of the Society of Architects of the United Kingdom.

Although his public duties made heavy demands on Silvanus, they were satisfying to him. He was very upset when he was not elected mayor of Truro in 1903 but, according to his assistant, Alfred Cornelius, he really started to decline after attending the architects' dinner in London that May, when someone else was elected President and he was thanked for all that he had done during his time in office. Could it be that he felt his prestige slipping; was he afraid he was being eclipsed? Or was an overload of work precipitating a nervous breakdown? Perhaps a combination of all these contributed to his decline, pushing him into a dark world of depression, where he became reclusive, over-anxious, absent-minded, and paranoid. Having to attend the funeral of his uncle seems to have been the last straw, but his actions, including the acquisition of the revolver, were clearly predetermined. Silvanus had made his mark in death as well as in life.

The legacy of this talented but troubled man lives on. Schools, libraries, hotels and many other buildings across the Cornish countryside will long continue to bear witness to the bright lad from Luxulyan and the significant contribution he made to tourism and the culture of the county.

THE SECRETS OF
TINTAGEL

Nature must have been in one of her more whimsical moods when she created the awe-inspiring landscape around Tintagel, with its high and mighty coastline, topsy-turvy contortions, dark secret caves, deep wooded valleys and craggy winding inlets. Not surprisingly, this is a landscape heavy with mysticism and steeped in folklore and legend. People have always sought to understand and master their environment, dreaming up stories to explain the inexplicable, which became embellished over centuries of telling and re-telling.

Some of Cornwall's most colourful and enduring myths and legends are centred around the bold and striking headland of Tintagel Island, which has stood as a natural fortress since time immemorial. These tales, with their roots in oral history, seem to have filled the void left by the scanty documentation of the post-Roman period known as the Dark Ages. The legends of Mark, his nephew Tristan and the beautiful Yseult that were carried around the western coasts of Britain by ancient mariners were associated with Tintagel. Tristan came to be associated with the 6th century figure Drustan, the son of Cunomorus, and as time went by Cunomorus came to be identified as the mythical King Mark. By the time these stories were written down, the court of King Mark had been placed at Tintagel.

The most celebrated and romantic tales were woven around King Arthur and his Knights of the Round Table, with their ideals

King Arthur. (Sketch by Jenny Morgan)

of chivalry, gallantry and courtly love. According to tradition, Uther Pendragon, King of Britain, invited the Cornish Duke Gorlois and his beautiful wife Igraine to a splendid feast at Winchester, but when it became apparent that Pendragon had taken a strong fancy to his lady, the duke hastened back to Cornwall and hid her in the castle at Tintagel. Not to be thwarted, the enamoured king set off in hot pursuit and dispatched Duke Gorlois. Then, with the assistance of Merlin the wizard, he disguised himself as the duke and gained access to the marital bedchamber. The baby that the duped wife subsequently bore was taken away by Merlin and handed over to a knight, whose wife nursed him at her breast along with her own son. He was christened Arthur. Throughout his formative years he was instructed in worldly wisdom and groomed in knightly accomplishments by the wizard, who as the son of a Christian mother and a demon, bridged the divide between the pagan and Christian worlds.

It was Arthur's destiny to become a much admired king and a romantic hero of generations to come. He assisted damsels in distress, freed wronged captives and engaged in a host of other chivalrous exploits in the grand heroic traditions of knight errantry. As a warrior king wearing a coat-of-mail and carrying a shield bearing the image of the Virgin Mary he led his army into many battles. One of his most magnificent swords, which shone with the intensity of thirty gleaming torches, was obtained from the Lady of the Lake in spectacular style, with a little guidance from Merlin. It emerged eerily from the midst of the lake, held aloft by a graceful arm clad in a white silk glove. If swords loomed large in Arthur's life, that is the way it was in those times. They were symbols of manhood and power, often associated with the supernatural. According to tradition, they were discovered at the bottom of lakes, having been cast at the beginning of a reign and yielded to the waters at the end.

Merlin was also influential in Arthur's acquisition of the magical round table, when he married fair Guinevere. Only virtuous knights were allocated a place at this elite table, where their names were elegantly written out. Should they fall from grace, their names just disappeared. Their preoccupation with pursuing the Holy Grail (the cup used by Christ at the Last

Supper) weakened their military stance and helped to bring about their downfall.

Mordred, the nephew of King Arthur, assisted by Saxon invaders, advanced on the king's army. The bloody battle which ensued resulted in Mordred's death and Arthur's mortal wound. Although it was said that 'the grave of Arthur no man knows', some would site it at Slaughterbridge, on the upper reaches of the River Camel, and others at Glastonbury. Another version of the Arthurian legend says that he was reincarnated as a chough, and would one day return to his Cornish kingdom and lead his people into a wonderful age of peace and plenty. Strange to say, these crows with their red legs and curved beaks, which are featured on the Cornish coat-of-arms, have recently reappeared on the Cornish cliffs after an absence of nearly 50 years.

Stirring tales of King Arthur and his heroic struggle against the ruthless Saxon invaders featured widely in the songs of strolling minstrels in medieval times. But where did these tales come from? Who was King Arthur?

It was the 12th century historian Geoffrey of Monmouth who linked the mythical King Arthur with the magnificence and splendour of Tintagel Castle. In compiling his history, he drew on earlier works in which a Christian warrior triumphed in battles against the pagan Saxons. Although he cited Tintagel simply as the place where Arthur was conceived, subsequent writers saw the castle as a fitting birthplace for the celebrated monarch, including the 17th century historian John Norden, who stated that 'the famous Arthure, Kynge of the Brytons, was here begotten in this castle'. Malory's *Morte D'Arthur*, dating from the 1460s, went so far as to say: 'Then when the lady was delivered, the King commanded two knights and two ladies to take the child, bound in a cloth of gold . . . the child was delivered unto Merlin, and so he bore it forth unto Sir Hector, and made an holy man to christen him and named him Arthur.' The poet Alfred Tennyson rekindles the famous saga in the 19th century with his epic *Idylls of the King*. Although the greatly romanticised interpretation of the story, linked with the supernatural powers of Merlin and the wonderful sword Excalibur, caught the imagination of the public and exploded into a lucrative Arthurian industry, it tended to be dismissed by others, who pointed out that at the time of the supposed King Arthur the medieval castle was not built, dashing suits of armour had yet to be invented, and the supernatural elements were mere fiction. So is there any evidence that King Arthur ever existed?

The whimsical world of fable and romance is usually far removed from that of down-to-earth scientists, but ongoing archaeological discoveries have brought them closer together in the context of Tintagel where a pattern emerges into which someone like King Arthur might well have fitted during the obscure period of the Dark Ages. The Romans left some intriguing evidence of their association with these parts, including two milestones. One was serving as a coffin rest and whetstone for reaping hooks at the lower entrance of Tintagel churchyard until 1889, when a perceptive observer caught sight of an inscription thrown into relief by the angle of the setting sun. This connected it with Caesar Gaius Valerius Licinius and dated it to around AD 250. A second milestone was being used as a gatepost at Trethevy, 1½ miles to the north-east, when it was discovered in 1919. It bore an inscription to Galius and Volusian, who reigned briefly between AD 251 and 253. The milestones and more recent discoveries of coins and imported pottery dating from the third and fourth century suggest that the headland of Tintagel was a focal point of some importance in Roman times, recognised by the imperial authorities, and serving perhaps as a local tax centre.

The departure of the Romans left Britain vulnerable to attack, and some authorities believe that the Dark Age warrior hero who eventually stemmed the Anglo Saxon invasion may well have been King Arthur, or some mighty leader on whom the legend of Arthur was based. A 6th century British monk called Gildas mentioned a battle in which the Britons crushed the invading pagans, without naming the leader who must have led them to victory. One modern expert remarked, 'There is an Arthur-shaped hole in the heart of 5th century Britain. If the legend had not been written, you would have to invent it to make sense of the period.' Could this Dark Age hero's life be the basis of the fabulous legends of King Arthur?

Extensive archaeological discoveries of the 1990s revealed that the headland of Tintagel was probably a royal stronghold and place of some importance at that time, with cultural and trading links with Byzantium, rather than a monastery, as earlier historians had suggested. The Roman presence left a prestigious stamp on the exposed clifftop site, and when Cornwall became part of the Westcountry kingdom of Dumnonia the choice of Tintagel as a royal seat for kings visiting this part of their domain may have been influenced by a desire to harness some of this glory. Excavations have revealed larger quantities of pottery and other artefacts relating to immediate post-Roman times than have been discovered elsewhere in Britain, and the rarefied nature of these imported goods would suggest that Tintagel was once the scene of lavish hospitality and grand ceremonial in the style of ancient Rome. Trading vessels would have unloaded in the natural little haven at the foot of the cliffs between the Island and Barras Nose, with the seabound site offering its own security. Might not a seasonal palace in such a magnificent setting have been the birthplace of a future king, as the legends suggest?

At some point in the 5th or 6th century, a decision had been made to reinforce the Island stronghold by excavating an enormous ditch along a natural fault line and constructing a defensive wall with the material, which may have given rise to the name Din Tagell, indicating a fortress (*din*) with a narrow entrance (*tagell*). Geoffrey of Monmouth described this constricted access rather fancifully as being 'through a strait rock, which three men shall be able to defend against the whole power of the kingdom'. It is not surprising that this impressive site, surrounded by colourful legends, was harnessed by successive seekers-of-power.

Perhaps it was a desire to be associated with the legendary heroic and idealistic splendour which had fallen on Tintagel's earlier castle walls, that influenced Earl Richard's decision to construct a new castle here in 1233. By that time, the famous Arthurian fable had been much embellished and the ambitious Earl, who was the brother of King Henry III, may well have felt that a castle on this prestigious site would enhance his image here and in Europe. The builders of the castle embarked on a very comprehensive plan, sweeping away former structures and replacing the ruined defences with mighty stone walls and battlemented towers.

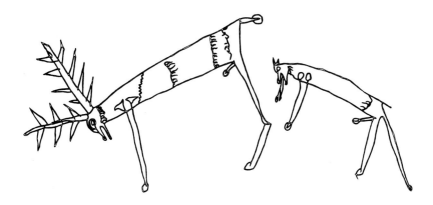

This archaeological graffiti dates from the 14th century and depicts a stag being chased by a dog. (Carl Thorpe and the Cornwall Archaeological Unit)

Drawings on slate discovered in the vicinity of the ancient isolated clifftop parish church provide a welcome insight into earlier days. These fascinating graffiti slates include an illustration of an armed warrior, various board games, and a turtle and other stylised creatures. In days of yore, churches were the focus of social and recreational activities, with fairs and festivals, dancing, games and plenty of eating and drinking. Pottery was smashed as part of the burial ceremonial, and traces of hemlock seeds revealed in analytical research suggest the taking of drugs. This partially excavated area around the island and the old parish church must have many more secrets to reveal.

There was great excitement in August 1998, when archaeologists found what was thought to be a 6th century slate bearing a Latin inscription with the name Artognou. It became known as the 'Arthur Slate' and was hailed by some as 'the find of a lifetime', in that it demonstrated that there was a high ranking person of that name at Tintagel, enhancing the age old Arthurian legend, and strengthening the idea that this was indeed a royal stronghold in the Dark Ages. Others said that it could have been written by a Roman citizen or a member of the clergy, or dismissed it as being only the latest in a long list of expert – confounding and tantalising developments which have kept the myth alive. A shopworker from Plymouth claimed to have etched it out while on a school trip to Tintagel as a 10 year old boy, copying the words from a book. However, the archaeologists smartly countered his claim, saying that it had been authenticated by experts and that the layers of undisturbed earth above fixed it at that date. Another expert described it as 'a cheeky piece of graffiti', which would find a place in posterity, as it was lettered in Latin in two or three different styles.

An early 20th century guidebook reflected on the historic mouldering stones recalling the romantic stories of King Arthur and his stalwart knights that allowed us to build 'castles in the air', bright with the pageantry of ancient days, re-echoing the wild music and clanking harnesses of warriors. The enchanting Arthurian tales of bravery, loyalty and other admirable qualities associated with the quest for spiritual purity, sometimes thwarted by jealousy, lust, betrayal and other human weaknesses, have struck a chord with humanity for centuries. They enrich our lives, create a yearning for a real or imaginary vanished age of style and splendour, and provide us with heroes. And in this day and age, we need heroes.

MYSTERY AT
SKINNER'S BOTTOM

In January 1920, the tranquillity of daily life in the tiny, scattered hamlet of Skinner's Bottom, a few miles from Redruth, was shattered by a particularly brutal double murder which claimed two of its well known inhabitants. 'How could anything so terrible have happened in a sleepy little place like this?' everyone wondered.

Jack Pryor, from nearby Mount Hawke, had gone to see a cattle dealer named Joseph Hoare on a business matter. He called out to Joseph, who was also an old friend, in his usual way as he approached the cottage at 9 o'clock on that fateful Sunday morning. Not getting the customary cheerful response, he peered over the garden wall and was shocked to see the buxom housekeeper in her nightdress lying face downwards by the cottage door. She was horribly battered about the head and bleeding from her injuries. Fearful of the dangers which might still be lurking, Jack Pryor rushed to the house next door to seek help.

The neighbour's wife, who suffered from a heart complaint, was all of a tremble when she heard the dreadful news. Her husband, her son and Pryor decided that they ought to put the situation in the hands of the police. Pryor returned to the scene of the crime with PC Stephens of Blackwater, and they found the critically injured woman attempting to get up on her hands and knees. Then they came upon Hoare himself lying battered by the garden gate and bleeding from horrific head injuries. He was fully dressed and clasping an old sack around his head with both hands. He was still alive – but only just. After helping to carry the two desperately ill people into the cottage, Pryor went to fetch the doctor from Chacewater, while the policeman rendered whatever first aid he could. Despite his efforts, they both died without regaining consciousness. When he arrived, Dr Forsyth made a superficial examination of the bodies and later carried out a post mortem, which revealed that both had received very severe head injuries resulting in fractured skulls. The murder weapon was a spiked fir branch weighing about four pounds, which was discovered about 20 feet away from Hoare.

The dilapidated little four room cottage where the tragedy occurred stood on its own in a secluded situation adjoining the road; it was not overlooked by any neighbouring dwelling. Passers-by had noticed that the lights were out at about 10 o'clock the previous night and assumed that the couple had gone to bed. PC Stephens observed that the unmade bed had been recently occupied by two people. One of the neighbours had heard Hoare's dog barking loudly at about 7.15 am on the Sunday morning, but did not attach any importance to it at the time. The branch which had been used as a murder weapon had probably been taken from the pile of firewood kept behind the cowhouse. Bloodstains on the side of the cowhouse and on the door, and the big pool of congealed blood, which Hoare must have lost after he fell, bore witness to the violent struggle which had occurred in the humble little cottage garden. The smears of blood found on a corrugated iron section of the cowhouse gave rise to speculation that the victim had tried to hoist himself up by pressing himself against it, and had staggered to the spot where he was discovered in an attempt to reach the cottage. Blood was also spattered around the spot where the woman was found. Who could have committed such a brutal crime, and what was the motive? These were the questions which baffled the police, and rumours abounded.

One theory was that the couple had had a quarrel and inflicted the wounds upon each other, but the fact that only one weapon was employed seemed to discredit this idea. On previous occasions Hoare had told his friends that he had been robbed. Had someone been lying in wait at the wicket gate? It seems that the most likely explanation was that the dealer had come down at the usual time to tend his stock when someone attacked him; when Mrs Sara, his housekeeper, came out in her nightdress to see what all the fuss was about, she was similarly set upon to ensure that she could never reveal the attacker's identity. If this was the case, was robbery the motive for this awful crime? Most of Hoare's money was kept in a bank account, and the rest of it was secreted in a bag about his person or at various places in the cottage, but the empty bag in his waistcoat was still buttoned up and large quantities of money remained around the house. Could this have been someone with a grudge who chose to seek a terrible revenge?

Hoare was a well liked, amiable sort of fellow; he was well known at Truro Cattle Market and most of the fairs and markets across Cornwall and Devon and was fond of a drink or two. Laura Sara, who had lived apart from her husband for the last 20 years, could be aggressive and had once struck her mother over the head with a big stick. She was also inclined to hit the bottle, but neither had been drinking the night before the tragedy.

The spotlight fell on the private lives of the ill-fated couple, and it emerged that Laura Sara had become the mother of six children during the eight years she had spent with her husband Hugh. All but one of their children had subsequently died, and he had gone off to America and started a new family with another woman. A few years earlier Sara had been convicted of assisting in keeping a disorderly house in Truro, and Hoare, who had previously been living with a brother and sister at Penstraze, was in the habit of associating with loose women. In fact her easy virtue and his sexual freelancing had been the common factor which brought them together. They began cohabiting in Truro, and had then set up home at Skinner's Bottom. To all outward appearances, they were living happily together. He loved and cared for her, and had told his friends that she was 'clean and all that a man could wish for'. He trusted her despite her drinking habits and had made out a will in her favour, dated 10th June 1918 signed with a cross as the mark of 'Joseph Charles Hoare'. For her part, there was a general feeling that she may have been taking advantage of his love and protection, for it was well known that she was associating with other men. This gave rise to speculation about Sara, and her men friends or even her estranged husband having a desire to get their hands on Hoare's estate. The crime scene swarmed with local policemen of all ranks, but their probing failed to throw any further light on the situation. In the end a decision was made to call in the experts from Scotland Yard, and everybody was in a state of high anticipation, waiting for the elusive breakthrough.

During the inquest, held in the little vestry adjoining the Wesleyan chapel, in the presence of Colonel Prothero Smith, the Chief Constable of Cornwall, Chief Inspector Heldon and Detective Sergeant Canning of Scotland Yard and other members of the police force, the coroner, Mr E.L. Carlyon, described the circumstances in which the bodies were found, and Dr Forsyth provided the medical evidence. Edwin Hoare identified the body of his brother and that of the woman. The coroner told the jury that he would not be going into the facts that day, but they would see that they must come to one of three conclusions:

'That either it is a case of one of the deceased parties having murdered the other, and then committed suicide, or there must have been a struggle between them and they both dealt each other such injuries that they subsequently both died; or the blows must have been inflicted by some third person.'

Then he adjourned the inquiry until such time as the police had ascertained by whom those injuries were caused.

No further light had been thrown on the mystery as to how Joseph Charles Hoare, aged 57, and Laura Sara, aged 45, had met their deaths when the adjourned coroner's inquiry took place at Blackwater Institute, although a witness said that he had seen Hoare clearing stones from a field on the Friday afternoon, and both of them engaged in the same task the following afternoon. Jack Pryor was taken to task by the coroner for not trying to help the injured woman before going for assistance.

'Why did you not go to her?' he asked.

'Because I was afraid.'

'What of?'

'I thought Hoare had gone mad and hit her, and thought that he might do the same to me.'

'You have known Hoare for many years. Do you think he was a person who was likely to go mad?'

The Cornish police and experts from Scotland Yard at the scene of the murder, Skinner's Bottom, January 1920. (Royal Cornwall Museum, Truro)

'No.'

The coroner suggested that he was afraid to enter the garden because he might be implicated in the murder. Pryor denied this, pointing out that he did not know what had happened, and did not want to go in alone. The coroner thought it outrageous that the two neighbours had not offered to return to the garden with him to help the victim as best they could. Pryor said he thought he ought to send for the police, but the coroner said the police might be miles away, whereas they were on the spot, and rebuked them for their conduct. A juryman intervened and suggested that the three men were so afraid that they did not know what to do, but the coroner maintained that they should have rendered first aid before summoning the police. Pryor said that Hoare was a 'jolly sort of fellow, who would not do anyone any harm, but he was somewhat addicted to drink.' Mr Tonkin, the next door neighbour, who was chided for his incomprehensible conduct in not attempting to help the injured woman, also spoke of Hoare's cheerful and easy-going disposition. There was a moment of drama during the course of police evidence, when the dead woman's bloodstained and muddy nightdress was produced, and examined by the jury.

The anticipated climax came towards the end of the proceedings, with the results of Scotland Yard's investigations. The two detectives had been carrying out exhaustive enquiries since their arrival on the 27th January, and Mr Carlyon smoothed the way by explaining that statements given before a coroner's jury might be accepted as evidence, although they would not necessarily be accepted as evidence in a police court or at the Assizes. Chief Inspector Heldon stated that he had heard a number of rumours, which he had dismissed. Robbery had been suggested as a possible motive, involving some third party lying in wait at the gate, but he could not accept this because there was no evidence that any money had been taken, and no one had been seen lurking near the house. As to speculation about jealousy being the motive, this theory was exploded because there were no concrete facts – just theories. Then he went on to outline his own theory . . .

After a great deal of thought he had come to the conclusion that the murder was committed by the one on the other, the woman assaulting the man in the first place. He suggested that although the relationship was apparently a happy one, and that Hoare had loved the woman, Sara only used him as a means to an end; that end being to obtain possession of his estate. She would have known about Hoare's will, leaving all to her, and that he had £200 in the bank and stock worth £150. It was common knowledge that Sara had led a loose life for many years, and someone like that would not take kindly to a hard and lonely life on a smallholding. She would be missing the questionable attractions of the public house, and the society of the dubious men associated with such goings-on. Hoare was not a young man. 'What was more feasible than the woman, tired of the humdrum life she was compelled to live, thinking to herself on that fatal morning, "Here is my opportunity, I will kill him, jump back into bed, and if anyone comes I can say I know nothing of it"?' He said that it would be an easy matter for her to do this. It might be assumed that she watched him dress himself, perhaps tying the sack around his shoulders, and peered through the window as he made his way to the cowshed. Warming to his theme, the detective went on to suggest that she slipped downstairs in her bare feet, grabbed a piece of firewood, and as he turned towards her dealt him a devastating blow on the forehead. She was a powerful woman, fully capable of making such an attack. Having received such a blow, Hoare would have wrenched the stick from her grasp and struck her two or three times, but missing her on the next attempt, the weapon flew out of his hands and landed where the investigators subsequently found it. The detective had been putting this theory to the test, positioning himself where he assumed the victim to have been, and aiming blows at an imaginary person. When he let fly with the stick it had landed remarkably near the same place. The amount of congealed blood found on the side of the cowshed suggested that he had initially fallen there, before staggering a few feet and collapsing. Chief Inspector Heldon said that this state of affairs demonstrated that the first blow that Hoare received did not render him incapable, as he had groped his way for three or four yards, passing through the gate into the garden. He submitted that, in the absence of any evidence to the contrary being discovered, his theory was the only feasible one. However, this cut no ice with the man who had carried out the post mortems.

Dr Forsyth of Chacewater said that Hoare had been struck a single blow, fracturing the frontal bone into five pieces. This had been a single traverse blow. When he was asked if the woman was capable of delivering such a blow, he said that she was physically strong enough to do so. But he did not think it was possible for her to have done so after being injured herself. Nor did he think it possible for the man to inflict such injuries on the woman after being dealt such a serious blow, although there had been instances of people doing remarkable things after sustaining fractured skulls and brain injuries. The woman had an abnormally thick skull, but had received two or three much harder blows, causing more extensive injuries.

During his brief summing up, the coroner said it was for the jury to decide who was right – Inspector Heldon or Dr Forsyth. It took the jury less than half an hour to agree – by a majority of 8 to 7 – that it was a case of wilful murder by some person or persons unknown.

'A Motive is a State of a Man's Mind'

Life had never been easy for Philip Davis or Wilhelmina Blee, and their wedding at Exeter in March 1931 did not mark the beginning of a marriage made in heaven. At the age of 27 Wilhelmina was relieved to have gained a ring on her finger, a provider and an improved status, just as her mother had been before her when she left the north of England to enter domestic service, and met and married carpenter John Blee of Hayle. Philip Davis, who also hailed from the north and was three years Wilhelmina's junior, had served in the army in India before setting up home with his bride in rented rooms in Market Street, Hayle. If their northern roots provided some sort of common background, their temperaments did not, for he was methodical and hardworking, and tried to maintain a smart appearance, while she became increasingly overweight and lethargic after the birth of the two children. Her inclination, borne of ill health, to lounge in bed instead of preparing the meals and doing the housework, was seen as laziness by her disgruntled husband, who was not exactly a ray of sunshine at the best of times. They had terrible rows, and Wilhelmina's financial security evaporated when her husband walked out on her. This left her very isolated, for, although she had been well known locally since her childhood days at Copperhouse School, her husband liked to maintain their privacy. He was seen as a rather remote figure, outwardly pleasant, quiet and reserved, well mannered and reasonably well educated, who sometimes went to the pictures. But they did not have any friends, and tradespeople were the only callers.

Davis left his wife in 1935, but if he thought that his domestic troubles were over, he was very much mistaken. She had sought police assistance and he was traced to Coventry and brought back to Cornwall under a warrant for maintenance. He resumed living with Wilhelmina but there was further trauma when both children sickened and died. Then life dealt a cruel blow to Wilhelmina's sister, Norah, whose husband died, making it necessary for her to take a live-in post as a domestic worker at an Exeter hospital, where it would be impossible to accommodate her 15 year old daughter Monica, and where she was known as 'Miss Blee'. So it was arranged that Monica would lodge with her aunt and uncle in Hayle, while her mother paid £2 a month for her keep. The teenager was tall for her age, and whereas Wilhelmina was of extremely ample proportions, Monica was very thin. She was rather immature, and liked to play with children's dolls, but her presence livened up the Davis household, even bringing the semblance of a smile to the breadwinner's usually gloomy countenance. On the face of it, things were on a reasonably even keel, even if Davis was frustrated about the lack of regular employment.

Christmas 1936 marked a turning point in the family's fortunes. Perhaps it offered some respite for the mismatched couple when the ailing Wilhelmina was carted off to Penzance for a lengthy spell in hospital. As far as Davis was concerned, things began to pick up when he found himself a well-paid job as a turner at the Climax Rock Drill & Engineering Works at Carn Brea, working on the night shift. At the beginning of January 1937 he and Monica moved into a spacious house in Tuckingmill. It was a short walk from the works, convenient for the pub and the general store which was run by his new landlord, Mr Andrew. He settled in well, but kept himself to himself, preferring to smoke and read books during the brief breaks at the factory, rather than enjoying the cheerful camaraderie of his fellow workers. They thought he was a bit odd, but his superiors considered him to be a good worker. The cosy domestic set up established during her absence came as a bit of a shock to Wilhelmina, on her release from hospital some weeks later. The neighbours saw very little of her

The main street through Tuckingmill today.

during this difficult period of adjustment, although she and Monica sometimes called at the shop down the street.

Davis routinely left home for the night shift at about 10 pm and returned at 8 o'clock in the morning; so he was usually at home during the day, snatching a few hours' sleep.

When the landlord called round to carry out some repairs on the chimney around midday on Thursday, 22nd April, he met Davis at the front door looking particularly haggard and drawn. He asked Mr Andrew whether he might rent the adjacent garage, which was separated from the house by a wire fence. 'Oh, I'm not sure about that,' said the landlord. 'I like to store my things in there. You never mentioned being interested in the garage when we were negotiating the rental of the house. It's worth a lot to me. I doubt if you'd be prepared to pay the sort of rental that I'd expect.'

'You told me I could rent the garage for £9 a year,' insisted Davis.

'I don't remember that. Why do you want it, anyway?'

'I'd like to use it as a workshop, and keep my lathe in there.'

'Well, I'll have to think about it,' said Mr Andrew.

Davis had never taken much notice of Mr Simpson, his next door neighbour, although they worked alongside each other on the shopfloor. So that gentleman was rather taken aback when he requested a private word in his ear during the night shift, on April 23rd. Davis certainly looked shattered. He had been smoking even more heavily than usual and had fallen asleep over his lathe during the refreshment break, which he had never done before. 'It's about my wife,' he explained. 'She's left me. She's gone off with Monica, and taken a lot of my money with her. I went to bed at about two o'clock yesterday afternoon, and when I got up to get ready for work, I found a note on the table saying she'd gone away and taken Monica with her.'

'Oh, I'm sorry to hear that, but I'm sure she'll be back. She'll come crawling back when the money's run out. Just you wait and see.'

'No she won't. She'll never come back. She said I would never see them again.'

'Well, where can she have gone? Does she have any relatives?'

'She's got a sister, Monica's mother, in Exeter, but they're not there. I mean the note said "don't bother to contact Norah, because we have no intention of going there." I am writing to my sister-in-law to ask if she would come and keep house for me. Do you think you could ask your wife if she would look after me? It would only be for a day or two, until Norah arrives.'

Davis was obviously not going to let the grass grow under his feet, for as soon as he finished the night shift, he turned up at the Simpsons' back door and asked Mrs Simpson whether her husband had told her his bad news. Mrs Simpson expressed surprise, commiserated with him, gave him a cup of tea and invited him to join them for breakfast. On hearing his sorry tale, she offered to help out until his sister-in-law arrived to keep house.

'No, no! You can't do that! I mean, I couldn't possibly put you to all that trouble. . . What I mean is. . . Well, the fact is I'd rather not go back there. I'd rather stay here.'

We can't put you up here,' spluttered Mr Simpson, 'because my father-in-law, Fred, sleeps in the spare room.'

'Well, I don't mind sleeping on the couch,' said the uninvited guest. The Simpsons were not at all happy about this, but he had a forceful way of putting things, and in the end it was agreed that he could catch up on his sleep in Fred Warrener's bed, which would be vacant during the day.

That evening Davis and his host attended a union meeting. After supper Mr Simpson got ready to go to work, but Davis started taking his shoes and socks off explaining 'I'm not going in to work tonight; I'm not feeling very well.'

'But I've already explained that we can't put you up. I'm very sorry about your domestic predicament, but I want you to return to your own home now,' stated Mr Simpson, in an attempt to put his foot down.

'But I'd rather stay here,' was the unexpected response. After further strained discussion, Fred Warrener tried to diffuse the situation by offering to share his bed with Davis that night.

As it transpired, Davis's sojourn extended to six days. He was not the easiest of visitors, and when he was not at work he hung around the house, getting under Mrs Simpson's feet, smoking, reading, brooding, and looking very depressed. He was reluctant to talk, and when Mrs Simpson tried to draw him out on the subject of his domestic troubles, she was surprised when he told her, 'I can't say I'm sorry she's gone. I've had a lot to put up with, with her. She's lazy and can't be bothered to get the meals or do the housework half the time.' The host family was puzzled by his odd behaviour, and could well understand his wife's desire to escape. The weekend was a particular trial for Mrs Simpson.

Although it may have seemed to the Simpsons that Davis had become a permanent fixture, never leaving their house, he made a few brief visits to his own. Having sounded out the landlord about renting the garage the previous Thursday, he called at the shop on the Saturday and was told that he could rent it for 4s 2d a week. Mr Andrew handed over one of the two keys, saying 'My son has the other one, so we'll hang onto it and let you have it after we have shifted all our stuff.' They removed most of their things over the next couple of days, then Davis turned up again, buttonholing the son and insisting that he hand over the second key, which he did. The following day Mrs Andrew asked if they could borrow it to enable them to get the rest of the clutter out of his way. He seemed rather agitated, saying that he would let them have it the next day.

On the day that Davis had obtained the second key from young Mr Andrew (Tuesday 27th), Mrs Simpson had noticed him cutting the wire fence between the back door and the garage. When they questioned him about this, he explained that he had done it to make a short cut for Mr Andrew. The next morning, after telling Mrs Andrew that he would be away for the day, he informed Mrs Simpson that he intended to do some gardening, to tidy things up before the arrival of his sister-in-law. He then spent about an hour moving earth and stones from the garden into the garage with the aid of a fire shovel and a bucket. Fred Warrener from next door called out to ask if he would like to borrow a spade but he declined the offer, saying he would get some proper tools at the weekend. Mr Warrener thought it very odd, and mentioned it to his daughter. After spending some time in the garage Davis returned to the Simpsons' house and had a rest.

At about 9.30 that evening he said he fancied a pint, and intimated that he was going down the pub for a drink. But he returned after about ten minutes, complaining that the beer had upset his stomach, and he didn't think he'd be able to get to work. But in the event he turned up for the night shift.

On his return from work on the morning of Thursday 29th, Davis called at the shop to hand over the spare key, saying that he had removed everything from the inspection pit for their convenience. 'Right you are. I'll be around later in the morning to collect it. I hear that your wife and niece have left you,' said Mr Andrew.

'Who told you that?' asked Davis sharply.

'Well, someone must have mentioned it in passing. They didn't come round to the shop at the weekend to pay the grocery bill, and they haven't put in an order for groceries to be sent up this week.' 'Yes, my wife and niece have gone away,' admitted Davis. 'They are gone away for good.'

'When the money is gone they'll be back,' said Mr Andrew.

'No, they will never come back. They have got all the money they want. They have taken a lot of money with them. They won't want no more. I'm hoping my sister-in-law will come down and housekeep for me.'

On leaving the shop Davis returned to the Simpsons' house, and sat down to write the long planned letter to his sister-in-law. It read:

Dearest Norah,

I have some startling news for you, and it is that Willie has left me and taken Monica with her, and she says I shall not find her through you, as she does not intend to correspond with you. She went last Wednesday night before I came down to go to work.

I am at present staying next door, and I want you to come, if you will be a dear, and look after me, as I think it will be much better for you than being morning and night up there.

You can have anything you want from me, as I have a good job, and am earning £4 a week. You can come down on Saturday and I will meet you at the station at Camborne.

I hope it is not too great a shock for you.

From your loving Brother.

P.S. Be a dear and write per return.

The letter was dispatched, and Davis went to bed, looking more relaxed than he had done since engineering his way into the Simpson household.

When Mr Andrew called round to collect the remainder of his property from the garage, he was astonished to find it ultra tidy, with no trace of the earth and stones that Mr Simpson told him about. Being curious, he started to remove some of the railway sleepers neatly covering the inspection pit, and discovered a large quantity of earth and rubble beneath. Thinking this very odd, he went next door to fetch Mr Simpson, and between them they lifted more of the sleepers from the pit, which was nearly five feet deep. Then Mr Simpson ventured down the stone steps into the pit, and scraped away more of the soil until he came across some sacking and rags. Then to his horror he unearthed a human hand, and the air was filled with a sickening stench. He leapt out of the pit, and they both had the presence of mind to replace some of the sleepers and lock the garage before notifying the police.

Superintendent Hosking arrived on the scene, along with Sergeant Rogers and Sergeant Stone. When Sergeant Rogers went into the garage and removed some more earth from the pit, he found a blanket and a sheet, then a portion of a human body, and it soon became apparent that Wilhelmina and Monica had been buried there. The two sergeants went to the Simpsons' house, where they found Davis apparently asleep in the bedroom. Sergeant Rogers shook him and said, 'Wake up. Are you Mr Davis?' He responded with a groan, signifying that he was. 'Get up and get dressed.' The superintendent called the sergeant away, leaving Sergeant Stone with Davis, who sat up and asked him what he wanted. 'We are making enquiries. . .' 'I know what you want. You know me and you know my wife,' he said, referring to their time in Hayle. After being cautioned he confessed: 'I done them both in with a hammer. I don't know what made me do it. I have been in a mental home. We had a row the night before, before I went to work.' On being told that he would be detained at Camborne Police Station on suspicion of having caused the women's deaths, Davis wanted to know what he ought to wear, as the clothes at the end of his bed were only working clothes. While he was dressing he told the sergeant, 'They didn't suffer. I hit them on the head with a hammer, and they are both out there in the pit. The hammer is in my toolbox at the works.'

At Camborne Police Station Davis started to say, 'You know my wife was a big person. . .' when Sergeant Stone cautioned him. 'I have been to a mental hospital,' Davis said. 'I suppose I must have been out of my mind. I have been to a mental institution, and my mother was mentally deficient, too. That is all I can think of.' A little later he mused, 'The only chance I have got is that I have been in a mental institution.'

Meanwhile, at the scene of the crime, Superintendent Hosking, Dr Hocking, the pathologist, Dr Blackwood, the Camborne police surgeon, Sergeant Rogers and a photographer were busy investigating a bloodstained shirt and jacket, which had been found inside the house, and a bloodstained towel, which had been washed out and hung up to dry. The bodies of Mrs Davis and Monica Rowe were found lying side by side beneath a dark blanket, with stones packed all around them. The area beneath them was stuffed with bedding and clothes. Mrs Davis weighed 16 stone so it would have been quite a daunting task to get her down the stairs and into the garage pit. Monica, who was of slight build and weighed under seven stone, was less of a challenge. Davis probably flung her over his shoulder, and the body remained in a curled up position in the pit.

Mrs Davis's head was wrapped in clothing, kept in position by a stocking knotted around the head, and another around her neck. Both wrists were bound with a strip of blanket. The bridge of her nose was broken, and she had a fractured skull, which was sufficient to cause unconsciousness, but probably not death. It was thought that she had been dead for about seven days, and that the actual cause of death was asphyxiation, which happened rapidly.

Monica was clothed in a vest and bust bodice, dress and dressing gown, and her body was covered with a coat. Her head was wrapped with the skirt of the dressing gown, secured around the neck with a tightly knotted stocking. When this was removed she was found to have a gag in her mouth, and her jaw was firmly closed by a leather belt fastened under her chin. She also had head injuries, likely to have caused unconsciousness rather than death and she had been suffocated. But death came to her rather more slowly.

It caused a tremendous sensation when news of the double tragedy began to filter out. Crowds hung around the garage where the bodies were found, and a constable remained on duty to prevent trouble. Many onlookers lined the streets of Camborne, and extra police were on duty outside the church of All Saints at Roskear, when the funeral of the victims took place. Large crowds also assembled outside Camborne Police Court, where Philip Edward Percy Davis was charged with the murder of his wife Wilhelmina Vernmadelle Davis and also with the murder of his 15 year old niece, Monica Rowe. He was remanded in custody at Exeter Prison. When he appeared at Camborne and subsequently at Bodmin Assizes, it was noted that he presented himself well, wore an overcoat and a well cut suit. His hair was neatly brushed and he stood smartly to attention and showed respect for the courtroom officials.

Davis had been represented by Mr Leslie Brooks, barrister-at-law of London, for the hearing at Camborne Police Court, where he pleaded 'Not guilty'. Mr D.R. Paling for the Director of Public Prosecutions had stated that 'a motive is a state of a man's mind. . .

If this man caused the death of these two women, he is the only person who knows why he did it.'

The courtroom at Bodmin Assizes was crowded, when the Tuckingmill murder charges were heard before Mr Justice Lawrence. Opening the case for the prosecution, Mr G. D. Roberts stated that on the night of 21st April or on the morning of 22nd April, the prisoner murdered each of these women, by firstly rendering them unconscious, and then asphyxiating them by tying something over their heads. Then he tried to conceal the evidence of his crime.

He recounted the entire sequence of events, and concluded by saying, 'He has a row with his wife before he goes to work. The hammer is kept at the works. When he goes back from work the next morning, he brings the hammer with him. He finds his wife in bed. He hits her on the head with a hammer. He renders her unconscious, and then there is asphyxiation. There is no explanation anywhere, of course, as to why the niece was murdered. You may think that if the prisoner had murdered one, he would have been driven by self-preservation, equally, to remove the witness of the crime. Had the wife been murdered, and the niece allowed to remain alive, she would have raised the alarm. and everything would have been discovered in a few minutes.' He had forced his way into the Simpson household to prevent Mrs Simpson from entering his home and making a grizzly discovery. It was thought that Davis moved the bodies from the house to the pit during the ten minutes he said he had been in the pub.

Mr J. L. Pratt, addressing the jury on behalf of the defence, said that what he would put before them would lead to one question, and that was whether or not, assuming this man murdered these two women, he was, at the time he did it, insane. The evidence that it was this man's hand that killed these women came from the prisoner's confessions. Could they rely on these confessions?

The evidence of the accused's father, Alfred Davis, a labourer from Northampton, who had not seen his son for 11 years, and his stepmother, Martha Louisa Davis, provided a powerful insight into a troubled family history. Alfred Davis said that Philip was the eldest of five children by his first wife, who became increasingly violent and obsessive after the births of each of the children, and spent some time in a mental institution. Her father, the prisoner's grandfather, had also had a violent temper and behaved strangely. The witness married Martha five months after the death of his first wife in January 1922. The father said that things began to change for Philip when the stepmother came on the scene. He said his son was apt to lose his temper when things did not go his way, and when they tried to confine him in his bedroom, he smashed the furniture and broke the lock on the door. He gained employment as a hallboy in 1924, but was brought home by the butler and footman six months later in a confused and rambling state. He was sent to a mental institution in August 1924, when he was 18, and certified insane. However, he was discharged as fit after four months, much to his stepmother's dismay. At the time of the trial his youngest brother was confined in a mental institution.

The deputy superintendent of the Northampton hospital had checked Davis's records, and having seen him just before the trial, had come to the conclusion that he was suffering dementia praecox, a disorder (now known as schizophrenia) associated with puberty, which could recur after periods of normality. Dr Richard Henry Blair, whose patient Davis had recently become, noted that, according to the records, the doctor who had certified him insane had done so on account of his rambling talk, strange behaviour and repeated attempts to interfere with his stepmother. Davis had accused the butler of molesting him, and most of his anxiety centred around sexual ideas. He was mesmerised by feelings of unworthiness and guilt, and the sinfulness of having started smoking at the age of thirteen. All this was consistent with dementia praecox. His behaviour in court supported this diagnosis.

Cross-examined by Mr Roberts, Dr Blair said that it would be his duty to certify Davis as insane. Health factors, financial problems and the loss of his two children would all have contributed to a flare up of his mental illness. He said that he would not have known what he was doing at the time of the attack. Mr Roberts harried the doctor regarding certification of the patient, suggesting that he had reached this conclusion too quickly. Dr Blair stood his ground on this, adding that Davis's lack of emotion during the trial was an indication of his condition.

Dr Josiah Carse, the deputy superintendent at Berrywood Mental Hospital in Northampton, made it clear that the background hereditary details of this case were of the greatest importance. The prisoner's sex life had been disordered from the age of 13, and he had been certified at the age of 18. He was of the opinion that the prisoner had been relapsing since December, and this culminated in an attack of complete confusion. Davis would not have known what he was doing when he attacked his wife.

This concluded the case for the defence. However, Mr Roberts sought to recall more evidence about Davis's mentality from the medical experts. Mr Palmer of Hayle said that he had known the prisoner for about five years, and had never noticed anything abnormal about him. Dr Griersen, senior medical practitioner at Brixton Prison, who had interviewed Davis twice at Exeter Prison, found the prisoner to be quite rational, and Dr Preece, the medical officer at Exeter Prison, had told him that Davis had not shown any evidence of mental disorder.

The judge took fifty minutes in his summing up. The jury was absent for about thirty-five minutes, and on their return they were all agreed upon the verdict: 'We find prisoner is guilty of murder,' said the foreman. Mr Justice Lawrence pronounced the death sentence and Davis was subsequently hanged at Exeter Prison.

Was this really a murder without a motive? Davis had murdered his wife, whom he despised, and disposed of his niece, of whom he was very fond. At the time of the murder Wilhelmina was in her night attire, and Monica was partially dressed. According to local tradition, Davis and Monica had become intimate while his wife was in hospital, and this had led to quarrels when she returned and realised what was going on. There had been a row before Davis set off for the night shift, and he returned with the hammer on that fateful morning. Had Wilhelmina caught him as he was having his wicked way with Monica? And had his original intention been to do away with her, giving him a clear field to continue living in sin with Monica? If his niece had become frightened and hysterical, he had to silence the only person he really cared for, in an attempt to save his own life.

THE BEAST OF
BODMIN MOOR

The legend of the Beast of Bodmin Moor has gained momentum in recent years, capturing the imagination of some, and being dismissed out-of-hand by others. When reports of wild cat sightings began to appear in the newspapers in the late 1970s, the witnesses were treated with scorn in much the same way as those who claimed to have seen the Loch Ness monster or alien space ships. Certain editors of national newspapers made sport of the subject, whereby country bumpkins from the whimsical land of piskies and fairies who fancied they had seen large wild cats roaming the countryside were daft, deluded, or had lingered too long at the pub.

While some reports were jokey and patronising, causing embarrassment to those involved, other journalists scrambled to produce lurid accounts of their own so-called encounters with the dreaded Beast on the 'killing fields of Bodmin Moor', which savaged the farm stock, and terrorised the moorlanders with blood curdling screams and howls of rage! Although this made for entertaining reading, it left a cynical legacy. However, the question remains. Are there big wild cats at large on the moor? If so, what is their species, and how did they come to be there? How would their presence affect the indigenous wildlife? Could they turn aggressive and become a danger to us?

Much of the evidence that we have today has been brought together by the *Western Morning News*, which has adopted a common sense, non-sensational approach to an issue of great concern to Westcountry farmers, with far reaching implications for those living in or visiting the area. This rational approach encouraged people who had been reluctant to divulge what they had seen, for fear of being ridiculed, to come forward and contribute to the paper's ever growing Big Cat Dossier. It emerged that 'A very significant number of sober, sane, sensible folk in the Westcountry have believed for a long time now that there are indeed wild cats out there, and that they are almost certainly breeding.' Thus Big Cat stories are no longer greeted with hoots of derision in the Westcountry, and many people are keen to find out more about them.

For those who have not experienced a sighting of these magnificent creatures, the topic is intriguing; for those who have, it is a serious business. I once saw a large black creature suddenly leap out of a wood and bound across the road with amazing speed and grace as I was taking photographs at Pantersbridge near St Neot in 1999. I have also seen an enormous paw print in a muddy track through the woods on Smallacombe Downs, just above Nine Stones Farm, where there have been a number of sightings and attacks on farm stock.

The generally accepted explanation for Big Cats roaming the countryside is that they are unwanted pets abandoned by their owners. In the 1960s and 1970s it became fashionable for people to keep exotic pets as status symbols. However, in 1976 the Dangerous Animals Act required such owners to either purchase expensive licences and keep them in secure compounds, donate or sell them to a zoo or have them put down. Some took the irresponsible and easy way out by releasing them into the wild, and leaving them to fend for themselves in an alien environment, where there were no natural predators to cull their numbers if they survived and bred. One man admitted to a wildlife expert that he had released two black African Golden Cats in this way, because they had become too unruly to control in captivity.

Some authorities maintained that there were already a number of cats in the wild, which had probably escaped from insecure zoos and menageries in Victorian times. Theories abound. The former Westcountry author Di Francis has been researching the subject of

The wild granite moors where the 'Big Cat' has been sighted.

Big Cats for over 25 years. She believes that an indigenous breed of large feline has been living in the wild since the Ice Age, and that sightings all over the British Isles have become more frequent in the last hundred years. She identified a photograph of a golden coloured Big Cat, published in the *Cornish Guardian*, as being of the 'Felis' family, which includes domestic cats and pumas, and another as a species 'not known in the world today'. The indigenous British cats are the size of pumas, with the bigger and more powerful males capable of not only dragging off, but actually carrying off a full grown ewe. Di keeps two black Scottish wildcats at her home, a species which scientists did not think existed until she proved them wrong. They originally dismissed her way-out theories but are now fully behind her research.

In the mid 1970s a down-to-earth forestry worker came rushing into Nine Stones Farm all-of-a-tremble, after seeing a tawny coloured puma-like cat about three feet long. He regretted reporting the incident, for it brought ridicule and unwelcome notoriety, and the whole situation resulted in him changing his job and moving away from the area.

Some years later the daughter of the household at Nine Stones saw a large black creature slope across the forestry track in front of her when she was out riding, but decided not to mention this to anyone. However, her father saw a similar creature a few days later and told her about it. After that it became commonplace to see fawn or black cats disappearing into the undergrowth. In December 1994 the same young lady got a good view of a large black cat moving along the foot of Hill Tor as she was feeding her horses. The creature paused, then sat and watched as one of her dogs started rushing towards it. She called it back, and the cat made off, leaping over a stream and a three foot hedge before disappearing into the undergrowth. She described it as 'the most beautiful thing I have ever seen', but she did not place it on record until December 1997, when reported sightings were being taken more seriously. There have been quite a few sightings around the area since then, with sheep and calves being savaged and their carcasses stripped out in a characteristic way on various occasions. The Big Cats seem to turn their attentions to farm stock when their staple diet of rabbits is in short supply. It has been noted that the number of reported sightings tends to increase when rabbits are plentiful.

The appeal for information by the *Western Morning News* has brought forth a number of other previously unrecorded sightings from the mid 1970s, including one on a narrow, constricted road between Pensilva and Lostwithiel late one night. The motorist said that he came up behind what looked like a puma. It ran in front of his car for quite a distance, and leapt away and disappeared as the roadside banks evened out. Several farmers from Goodaver, Common Moor reported they had seen big brown and black cats in the surrounding area, and said that the large cats were breeding on the moor. The cats' numbers would increase, as there was an 'endless parlour' of rabbits, foxes, sheep and calves. Perhaps this unlimited supply is just as well, as one Big Cat expert says that pumas 'prefer rabbits to people', but who knows what would happen if there were to be an unrestricted breeding boom, and the moorland larder ran short? Would they be tempted to add people to the menu?

A pet shop owner who also liked hunting rabbits claimed that he had 'spared the Beast of Bodmin', when he had a very close encounter with a black puma-like cat, with white flashings down its front, near Bastreet on the eastern side of the moor. Having sent his springer spaniel into some undergrowth to flush out the rabbits, he was standing by with his 12-bore shotgun when the startled creature emerged and bolted past him into an area of marshland. Although he said that he could easily have shot it, he did not wish to kill it, and hoped that no one else would want to kill it either. There have been no reported attacks on people so far, although in October 1993 a 37 year old woman claimed that a Big Cat leapt on her and knocked her out as she was walking her dogs on Bodmin Moor. The police investigated the case and a doctor confirmed that she had received a blow to the head and suffered severe shock.

For the farming fraternity, the fact that officialdom was slow to acknowledge the possible existence of big wild cats, which the farmers believed were responsible for savage attacks on their livestock, was very frustrating. However, they had an influential ally in North Cornwall MP Paul Tyler, who lived at Rilla Mill, on the edge of Bodmin Moor, where the Beast had been sighted just yards from his home. His lobbying led to the very first Beastly conference, where police, farmers and senior ministry officials put their heads together to work out a strategy. In January 1995 an inquiry into suspicious sheep deaths on the moor was set up by Agriculture Minister Angela Browning, and the press announced, 'Ministry men to go on the moor and look for legend.' Farmers were interviewed about unexplained sheep deaths, and photographs and videos of sightings were analysed in an attempt to weed out magnified photographs of pussy cats or other dubious pictures.

In the end, it was a situation where no one wanted to end up with egg on their face, and the rather dismissive conclusions were greeted with scorn and indignation by the farming folk, and dismay by others who had been concerned about the issue. The inconclusive study of 1995 was criticised as being underfunded, too short and woefully inadequate, leaving many questions unanswered.

The subject of 'The Beast' refuses to go away. Fleet Street journalists, big cat handlers, would-be hunters, local policemen and many others have been on its trail for some time. Those whose lives have been affected by the phenomenon have sometimes travelled overseas to widen their knowledge of the subject of Big Cats. PC Peter Keen, who investigated the case of the woman who claimed to have come face to face with the Beast after being knocked to the ground in October 1993, and has seen wild cats on the moor on various occasions, went to the forest mountains of Idaho and Montana to research the cougar (or puma). Rosemary Rhodes of Nine Stones Farm, who has witnessed a number of sightings, and whose stock has been savaged on various occasions, went to the United States to attend a conference on the subject. The failure of the Ministry to come up with answers has prompted various other investigations over the years, while MP Paul Tyler called on the Government to conduct a full inquiry.

One of the most basic methods of detection to be employed in recent times was the 'honey trap'. This involved placing a female puma in a cage positioned in a Big Cat moorland hot spot, and waiting for her charms to work their magic! This allegedly led to a pair of blue eyes gleaming in the darkness, but nothing more. Clearly it called for a more sophisticated approach. So in August 1999 a high-tech infra-red time-lapse camera was positioned in the roof of a barn, where there had been five recent sightings of Big Cats. The £1,500 video would be triggered if anything broke an invisible red beam. But nothing did. Three months later 2625 Squadron, Royal Auxiliary Air Force Regiment, based at RAF St Mawgan, experienced a very cold session on Bodmin Moor during the course of a high-tech, all night stake-out in an attempt to flush out the Beast. Nothing was to disturb any Big Cat on the prowl, and a young female reporter was warned not to wear perfume. There was to be no talking, no smoking and absolutely no rustling of crisp packets during this sensitive exercise. Chicken and lamb entrails were scattered across the terrain as bait, along with seismic sensory detectors, which would light up if a large animal passed over them. Twenty-four men occupied observation posts on the edge of woodland, in a field and on top of a hill with thermal imaging equipment and night vision goggles. But nothing showed up.

The moorland fringes are reckoned to be the ideal habitat for these mysterious, mainly nocturnal animals, which like plenty of woodland and cover, but by the end of the 1990s reliable sightings were extending to the the china clay country around St Austell, and less wild environments such as the Falmouth, Redruth and Perranporth areas, and even to Saltash and other fringe-of-urban districts. The clay workers are very protective of the beautiful Big Cats they claim to have seen in some disused, overgrown pits. The men watch the cats, while they demonstrate a nonchalant attitude towards such human intrusion. The sighting of a Big Cat has a profound effect on the witnesses. One lady from Perranporth described its 'lovely shiny coat and great sweeping tail', and added, 'It's one of those things that takes your breath away.'

Dedicated followers of the Big Cat cult felt heartened at the start of the new millennium, when a local vicar, who was also a police chaplain, spotted a majestic creature with a glossy black coat calmly crossing the road as he drove past St Stephen's golf course one morning, for it felt as if they had the reassuring backing of God and the law. 'It was a wonderful sight!' he declared. 'It was beautiful. Just beautiful.' Evidence of enormous paw prints and scattered sightings continue to be reported across an ever-widening area, whereby the legendary Beast of Bodmin Moor (and Dartmoor, and Exmoor) seems set to become the Beast of the South West, or perhaps the Beast of Britain. So at the end of the day what is it?

The overall evidence would indicate that more than one species is at large, ranging from fleet-footed golden cats to handsome, shiny jet black creatures, with long tails, about three feet tall and up to six feet in length. Experts reckon that there are at least four different species out there, including pumas, panthers, lynxes and leopards, which have probably been inter-breeding. There could be other species as yet unknown to science. A number of photographs of varying quality purporting to portray the elusive Beast have been published in recent years, some convincing, others less so.

There is no conclusive evidence of the existence of Big Cats in the wild so far. Only one thing is certain; the romance and allure of these felines will continue to be with us for many years to come.

Mad or Bad?

Anyone of a certain age with Cornish connections is likely to recall the dramatic Giffard double murder of 1952, spectacular in its awfulness. As the bizarre details of the horrifying case emerged, it seemed more like a scenario dreamed up by some drunken movie scriptwriter than reality. It hit the national headlines, and struck a chord of fatal fascination in households across the country in those generally law abiding, gentler times, when settled family life was at the basis of society. People who had holidayed in the area could not believe that their idyllic dreamland could be the setting for such a crime, while stunned locals could not credit what had happened in their midst.

The Giffards were a much respected family playing a prominent role in local and county life. They were well connected, and pillars of society. Surrey-born Charles Giffard was a well known St Austell solicitor, clerk to the St Austell magistrates, and former Under Sheriff of Cornwall. He had served with the Royal Flying Corps during the First World War and became Commandant of the Special Constabulary in the St Austell Division during the Second World War, a post which he held up to the time of his death. He was a very capable man, but one who could be somewhat dictatorial. It was said of his courtroom work that he did his duty with out fear or favour, and that he had an ever present anxiety that justice should be done. Charlie Giffard was a keen motorist, who carried on from vehicle to vehicle his car registration number, ERL 1; a number destined for notoriety. His charming Irish-born wife, Elizabeth, was three years his senior. She was a smart, attractive woman, very much involved with the Conservative Party's affairs in Cornwall, and an enthusiastic bridge player. When the couple first arrived in the county they lived in St Mewan parish, where their elder son, Miles, was born. Then the successful solicitor had a splendid house named Carrickowl (*sic*) built on the clifftop at Porthpean, where Miles and his younger brother Robin used to play in the meadowy copse on the headland and scramble around collecting seagulls' eggs. As with others of their class, they had nannies and were sent away to boarding schools.

The first inkling that anything was amiss in the Giffard household on Friday, 7th November 1952 was when the 21 year old live-in domestic servant Barbara Orchard came back after an evening out with her fiancé, John Vaughan. This had been her half day off, and she had left soon after serving lunch to Mr Giffard and Miles, now 26 years old and kicking over the traces, who had returned from London earlier that week.

When she got back at 10.30 that evening there was no one in, which was strange as she had expected her employers to be at home. She had been in the vicinity for about half an hour before going indoors and she had heard a car speed away and seen its lights. As she approached the house, she saw that the hall light was on, as usual, but that the garage light was also on. As she entered the house she noticed that the outdoor coat and picnic basket which Mrs Giffard had taken with her to Plymouth that morning were lying on a kitchen chair, and her handbag and shoes were on a chair in the hall. It soon became apparent that odd things had been going on in the kitchen. Some coconut matting covering part of the floor had been removed, a rubber mat was wet, and the floor was smeary, as if it had been hurriedly washed over. She saw what appeared to be bloodstains on the floor and on the cooker, and noticed that a scrubbing brush, usually kept outside the kitchen door, had been left in the scullery sink.

It was a bewildering situation, and she did not know what to do. Being concerned about no one being home, she telephoned two local hospitals to see if she could get any news, then sat pondering, and eventually went to bed and endured a sleepless night. In the end she got up and made her way to her fiancé's house, arriving there at

Miles Giffard's girlfriend Gabriel Vallance outside the Assize court in Bodmin in February 1953. (The Ellis Collection, Cornish Studies Library, Redruth)

about 5 am, and told him that she feared something terrible had happened. The worried couple told Harry Rowe, the gardener, that something strange and rather ominous had been going on at his employer's house, and he set off for Carrickowl to see what it was all about. He got there at about 8.20 am, and when he went to the double garage adjoining the side of the house, he found Mrs Giffard's Standard car was in its usual place; but her husband's black Triumph was missing. There was blood all over the place; the earthen floor was wet and muddy, and looked as if someone had been trying to brush it; when he opened the car door he found a lot of blood on the floor on the driver's side. Looking around he noticed that some chrysanthemums he had recently potted had been knocked over, and realised that a heavy metal wheelbarrow was missing. He followed a trail, apparently made by the wheelbarrow, down the path and out through the back gate to the clifftop beyond, with pools of blood along the way. By this time Barbara's fiancé had joined him, and went rushing off to fetch the police.

Sergeant Lovering of St Austell arrived on the scene at about 9.10 on that Saturday morning. He saw two large patches of blood between the garage and back door of the house, and footmarks in the passage leading to the kitchen. A portion of the wall at the rear of the house had been knocked off and a car door handle lay nearby, suggesting that a vehicle had been carelessly backed out of the garage during a hasty departure. He and the gardener followed the track leading from the garage and toolshed to a substantial gate opening on to a public footpath across the headland. There were bloodstains on the garden gate and along the path. The wheelmark and bloodstains led them through a small plantation of trees to a ploughed field. Here, they came upon a woman's black hat, a man's brown trilby hat, a brown leather wallet, some correspondence, a handkerchief, a bunch of keys and eleven shillings in silver and copper. Near the edge of the cliff they came upon a man's kid glove, and saw smears of blood extending over the edge of the precipice. The policeman leant over as far as he dared, and saw the body of a man spreadeagled on his back across a rock, with his head near the base of the cliff. A wheelbarrow was poised just above his head.

A police team led by Detective Superintendent Julian of Cornwall Constabulary headquarters at Bodmin and Superintendent Johns of St Austell converged on the scene, along with Dr Hocking, the county pathologist. A guard was put on the house and the area was cordoned off, while a detailed search was made and photographs taken. In the course of these investigations, it was confirmed that the body was that of Mr Giffard, and his skull had been so badly shattered in the clifftop fall, that his brains were spattered across the adjacent rocks. There was no sign of Mrs Giffard at first, but, after searching the shore, they came upon her body wedged amongst the rocks 95 yards to the west, where it would probably have been covered by the high tide of the previous evening. It was obvious that both victims had been dealt severe blows by a heavy instrument before being tossed over the cliff. Police threw a mantle of secrecy over the tragedy, and friends and colleagues of the deceased were unaware of what had happened.

Then, as news filtered out, rumours and counter-rumours flew in all directions. The hunt was on for Mr Giffard's Triumph and its driver, and a nationwide police message was sent out. The driver was thought to be Miles Giffard, and the police, who had obtained an address in London, had got in touch with Scotland Yard. The Flying Squad's discovery of a black Triumph with the registration number ERL 1 in Tite Street, Chelsea at midday led to his arrest ten hours later.

Miles was originally arrested on a holding charge of stealing his father's Triumph roadster on the Friday night. Around noon the following day (Sunday 9th), he was interviewed in London by Superintendent Lee, of the Metropolitan Police and Detective Superintendent Julian who had travelled up from Cornwall. He was told about bloodstains found in the car, and was asked to account for his movements since midday on Friday. If the police had thought that the suspected perpetrator of this heinous crime would be a hard nut to crack, they were in for a few surprises. The personable but immature young man responded by saying, 'I know what you are referring to. I wish to admit everything to you with as little trouble as possible, please. I had a brainstorm,' and went on to make a full confession.

A large crowd of curious onlookers, mostly female, awaited the prisoner's arrival at St Austell police station the following afternoon. They jostled for a better view as he was driven up in a black saloon car with steamed-up windows, seated between two uniformed officers. But they only got a glimpse of him in the fading light, and press photographers were thwarted by screening blankets in their efforts to obtain photographs of him. Within ten minutes a court assembled in the guardroom. This had been the domain of his father, Charlie Giffard, and the court paid tribute to the man who had been its clerk for the last twenty-three years. It was ironical that the clerk to the Tywardreath magistrates, taking over his role and standing where he normally stood, was reading out the charge to his son: 'That on November 7, 1952, at Porthpean in this county, you did murder Charles Henry Giffard.' Miles, who was wearing a fawn check suit and tartan tie, stood there looking tired, with his dark hair dishevelled. This son of a very wealthy family spoke only six words during the short hearing:

'May I apply for legal aid?' He was told that he could, but, in the event, his uncle, General Sir George Giffard, stepped in and assisted Miles in his defence. Mr W.G. Scown of St Austell, one of Cornwall's best known advocates, who had known the young man for several years, agreed to act on his behalf.

Representatives of the Giffards' far ranging business and social activities attended an impressive memorial service in the parish church, while two of Mr Giffard's brothers led the family mourners. The younger son, Robin, who worked on his uncle's farm in Kenya, had been informed of the tragedy by telegraph.

Those who had carried out the initial investigations at Carrickowl felt overwhelmed by the luxuriousness of the place in its idyllic setting overlooking St Austell Bay, and were puzzled as to how anyone fortunate enough to live there could possibly contemplate murder. But this situation was probably at the root of Miles's troubles, for it is not always easy for children from such a successful, affluent background to live up to their parents' expectations. Miles had excelled at sport, especially cricket, had played for the county and wanted to be a professional cricketer. But his domineering father wanted his elder son to follow in his footsteps and become a solicitor. The lad might have been better able to cope with life had he been born into a lowlier family, attended a day school, not had nannies, and later earned his own living.

Miles had been an outsider throughout his public school days, but developed an *esprit de corps* during the four years he spent in the Navy as a rating. However, this period of happiness came to an abrupt end when he returned home and worked in his father's dreary office in St Austell, studying law to qualify as a solicitor. He was not cut out for this sort of thing, and his failure to knuckle down to the task led to some serious disagreements between father and son. He gave up the struggle in November 1951, and when he came into a legacy of £750 shortly afterwards (worth many times that amount these days), he took himself off to Bournemouth. Having squandered the money away within four months, he went through a series of menial jobs including working for an estate agent in Ringwood and selling ice cream. He then 'scrounged around for a bit', before returning to Porthpean in June 1952.

There was no fatted calf for this Prodigal Son, and a couple of months later he took off for the bright lights of London and rented a furnished room at 5 Walpole Street, Chelsea. He had become a heavy drinker, living hand-to-mouth, borrowing money and bouncing cheques, after exhausting his father's regular allowance of £15 a month. During evenings at a public house in King's Road he was introduced to 19 year old Gabrielle Vallance. She and her mother took a liking to this handsome, slightly rakish young man with his boyish charm and made him very welcome on his frequent visits to their home over the next few weeks. Miles was bowled over by Gabrielle; she fascinated him. He fancied he had found true love, at last, and in an effort to impress he whisked her around the West End, living far beyond his means. When she started chiding him about his untidy appearance, he gave her to understand that his parents would be sending on some clothing. He was reluctant to leave Chelsea but he needed to get his hands on some cash, and on Friday, 31st October he told Gabrielle that he was returning home to get some clothes. He assured her that he would be back on the following Monday.

Miles hitch-hiked his way back to Cornwall, staying overnight in a rat-infested barn in Somerset, and reaching home on Sunday, 2nd November. His hopes for the future had been pinned on his father forking out some more money, but all his dreams were shattered when they had a terrible row, during which he was given an ultimatum. He was forbidden to return to London and told that he must settle down and resume his studies to become a solicitor in Cornwall. Failure to comply with this would result in his being cut out of his father's will. Miles was very upset, and phoned his girlfriend to tell her the bad news. He was not aggressive by nature, and in traumatic situations was able to blank out reality and retreat within himself, displaying little outward sign of emotion. His mother found him at the bottom of the garden the following morning when she went to feed the poultry, and took him indoors. Neither the maid nor the gardener realised that there was anything drastically wrong in the Giffard household at this time, although Miles had told the friendly Harry Rowe of some of his adventures, and made a wry comment about not being able to afford a packet of cigarettes.

Carrickowl headland, Porthpean, over which Miles Giffard cast the bodies of both parents in November 1952.

It would seem from the contents of a letter written on Monday 3rd and posted by the gardener, that Miles was prepared to toe the line at first. It began, 'My darling Gabrielle,' and went on to explain, 'What I was afraid would happen has happened. I have had the hell of a row with the old man, made far worse by the fact that, as usual, he is right. . .' (Did he mean that he recognised that he had been irresponsible, or was this a touch of irony regarding the paternal dogmatism?) He said how fed up and miserable he felt, having hoped to have seen her the next day and taken her to Twickenham. As things were, only 'God and the old man' knew when he could get to see her, and he added a characteristic throw-away remark to the effect that 'short of doing him in' he could see 'no future in the world at all'. Things were not really quite that bad, and there was a hint of self-recognition as the letter went on, 'He has stopped my allowance, anyway, is giving me a pint of beer and 20 cigs. a day, and has said, "No Pubs". No doubt your mother would approve. Give her my love and tell her when she sees me I shall be a reformed character (nominally anyway).' He was obviously worried about losing Gabrielle, and he touched on this in the last paragraph of his letter. 'Gabby, my sweet, I love you terribly, and it really is breaking my heart to leave you in that den of wolves there. God bless you and write to me soon and often. All my love, my precious. Yours, Miles.' He wrote on the top of the letter, 'Please be good 'cos I mind terribly.' Gabrielle was very disappointed at the news, and sensibly suggested that he should get an ordinary job in London so that he could become independent of his father. She also invited him to stay with them over Christmas, and signed off her return letter, 'All my love, sweetheart, X, Gabrielle.' Such warmth and caring was far removed from the atmosphere in the parental home at the time.

There were more letters and phone calls, and as the situation became a little more relaxed, with everyone making more of an effort to be co-operative, Miles began to entertain hopes of seeing his lady-love before too long. Gabrielle had said how much she was missing him, and had urged him to come up to London if he possibly could. She was very much on his mind; in fact he could think of nothing else. By the middle of the week he had decided to return to London the following weekend. As the week progressed he became obsessed with the importance of getting to London. Nothing else mattered.

On the Thursday evening his sociable mother was in her usual good spirits at a charity bridge drive in St Austell. She may have been experiencing problems with her car, for the next morning she drove off to a Conservative meeting in Plymouth in her husband's dashing roadster, while he and Miles trundled into town in her more mundane Standard. Miles returned home soon afterwards. Had they had words that morning? Father and son appeared to be behaving normally during their midday meal served by the maid, although they had little to say to each other. Mr Giffard returned to work in St Austell, and Miles found himself alone in the house when the maid departed shortly after 2 pm.

Who knows what things were going through Miles's muddled mind that November afternoon? At 5.30 pm he phoned Gabrielle to say that he would be coming up to London to do some business for his father, who had promised to let him use his car, but that he would ring again at 8.15 pm to confirm this arrangement. Then he knocked back half a bottle of whisky, which could have done nothing to straighten out his state of mind. It so happened that his father and mother arrived home within a few minutes of each other around 7.30 pm. Mrs Giffard went straight indoors while Mr Giffard remained in the garage, apparently doing something to the Standard car. Then Miles approached, and struck him over the head with one of the iron pipes which lay partially buried in the earthen floor at the side of the garage. The pathologist, Dr Hocking, who was also a family friend, thought his father may have been getting out of the car, or at any rate facing him, as the attack was made, and put up an arm to protect himself before slumping to the ground unconscious. Whereupon Miles headed for the kitchen and dealt his mother a blow from behind with the same instrument, knocking her out. Then a few minutes later, at about 8.15 pm, he made a second call to Gabrielle, telling her that he was definitely coming to London in his father's car, and asking if he could go to her house for a wash and a shave the next morning. He then returned to the garage, intending to take the car, and found his father coming round. So he hit him again with blows which were probably fatal, leaving a tuft of hair and a portion of scalp on the garage floor. When he rushed indoors to pick up some clothes he found that his mother was coming round so he struck her again, sending blood flying in all directions. He said in his confession, 'There was blood everywhere. I didn't know what to do. . . Everything went peculiar. I cannot account for my actions.'

Although Miles had said that he had taken his parents' bodies to the cliff edge one at a time to throw them over, a single track left by a heavily laden wheelbarrow down the garden to the wooden gate and beyond led investigators to believe that he had initially loaded both bodies onto the wheelbarrow. They could see where it had been tipped sideways to be manoeuvred through the gateway, and a bloodstained handkerchief found on the hedge suggested that he had wiped his bloody hands in order to get a better grip of the metal handles. There were indications of where he had paused to rest in the course of carrying out this gruesome task, and there was more blood near the cliff edge, where some of his parents' personal possessions were found. This was where he would have dumped his father's body, probably wishing to lighten his load. He trundled his mother a considerable distance through a copse and over a ploughed field in the darkness, flinging her over the cliff, hoping, perhaps, that her body would be carried away on the outgoing tide. The pathologist reckoned that she would have been unconscious, but still alive, at the time. Then Miles wheeled the empty barrow back to collect his father's lifeless body, rifling his pockets before lifting him back on the barrow. This time he took a shorter, easier route down a track to the sheer cliff edge above Duporth Beach, and cast man and barrow over the precipice. That anyone could have accomplished this act of desperation across extensive rough terrain in the darkness is astonishing. He had remarkable stamina, whatever his state of mind.

Miles must have been aware that the maid could return at any time as he went indoors and attempted to clean up the kitchen. He was still wearing his bloodstained clothes as he made his way upstairs and took items of jewellery and a box of sleeping pills from his mother's bedroom. (He later said that he had intended to commit suicide with the latter.) He also took some money from his father's coat pocket before packing a change of clothing, jumping into his father's Triumph car and heading off for London. The maid was in the vicinity with her boyfriend while this was going on and, had she returned a few minutes earlier, there might well have been a triple tragedy.

Miles had changed his clothes before reaching Okehampton, and threw his bloodstained trousers and jacket into the River Otter at Fenny Bridges just east of Exeter, along with the murder weapon. He added another bizarre twist to this tragic epic by picking up a couple of Cornish hitch-hikers near Ilchester. He told them he was going to see his girlfriend in Chelsea and chatted amiably with them. They thought he was 'a decent sort', but said that he was chain-smoking, seemed a bit preoccupied, and kept crashing the gears, When he dropped them at Chelsea Bridge, he said that he might see them on the road on Sunday night, when he would be returning to Cornwall, which seems to indicate that he was drifting in and out of a state of unreality. He then drove on to Tite Street, parked the car some distance from his girlfriend's home, and caught up on some sleep.

In those days, before the road systems were upgraded, the long drive to London was arduous at the best of times. The fact that he had driven through the night after such physical exertion and trauma, with little to eat, and arrived safely by about 6 am, is scarcely credible.

Miles emerged from the car at about 8 am, leaving the ignition key and some bloodstained shoes and clothing inside, and went to see Gabrielle and her mother. He stayed with them for about an hour, giving them to understand that he had left the car at a garage and was staying with relatives in St John's Wood. In fact he had booked into the Regent Palace Hotel, in the name of Gregory. He told them that he had a business appointment at 10 o'clock but would return for lunch, and headed off to Piccadilly Circus, where he managed to sell some of his mother's jewellery for £50. Later he phoned Gabrielle to say that he couldn't make it for lunch, but would meet her at 2 o'clock at Leicester Square. She turned up with her mother, and all three of them went to the Odeon cinema and saw the film *Limelight*. When they emerged, her mother returned home, while the young lovers went on a pub crawl.

Miles had seemed quieter than usual when he first arrived, but his tongue loosened up as the alcohol flowed. While they were in the Star at Chesham Mews, Miles asked Gabrielle to marry him, and she agreed but said that he would have to get a proper job first. He then confessed that he had done something terrible. 'What? Pinched your father's car?' she quipped. 'No,' he said, 'something worse than that.' They left the pub and shortly afterwards he told her that he had murdered his father and mother, and would not be able to see her again. She was very put-out and rather tipsy, but did not really believe him. They drifted on to the fashionable Thameside Prospect of Whitby pub at Wapping, and carried on drinking. They were well in the arms of Bacchus by the time Miles summoned a taxi, and on the way to Tite Street gave her his room number at the hotel and asked her to ring him the next morning. . .

After his arrest Miles freely admitted his guilt, but showed great concern for Gabrielle. In his statement he said, 'I want to be frank. I did it. I don't want Gabrielle brought into it. I want to tell you the whole story.' By a tragic irony, Gabrielle might well have turned out to be the making of this unhappy, mixed-up young man, providing the warmth and love he may never have previously known, which could have allowed him to develop a sense of responsibility and find his self-respect. After a two-day hearing in St Austell, the magistrates committed him to stand trial at Cornwall Assizes in Bodmin the following February. Newspapers reporting the drama included photographs of this particularly handsome family, with Mr Giffard looking smart in his police uniform, Mrs Giffard looking charming, with smiling Irish eyes, and Miles looking boyishly beguiling – the sort of son any parent would be proud to have.

At the Cornwall Assizes, Miles was charged with murdering his father, Charles Henry Giffard, at his home, Carrickowl, Porthpean, on 7th November 1952. When the case had been committed from the magistrates' court it had been intimated that one of the defences at his trial would be that on November 7th he was insane. According to the prosecution it was a premeditated murder, planned days in advance; Miles had made up his mind to go to London that day to meet his girlfriend, but as his father had refused to give him any money, and as he had no means of getting there, he had decided to murder his father in order to take his car.

Mr Maude QC, opening the case for the defence, said that although there was no doubt whatsoever that the young man killed his father and mother, and he probably knew a great deal of what he was doing, he had been 'gravely ill mentally' for many years.

Miles's former nanny, who described him as 'a lovely little boy', kind, loving, but very nervous, said he suffered from terrible nightmares. He would wake up screaming in fright, pointing at nothing and could be pacified only with difficulty. On occasions when she approached a room unheard, he would retreat into a corner, put his hands over his ears, and shout, 'No! Don't do it! Don't do it!' This behaviour was re-echoed during his unhappy schooldays at Rugby, when for no apparent reason he would throw himself on the ground and cry, 'Don't hit me! Don't hit me!'

Mr Justice Oliver at the time of the Giffard trial. (The Ellis Collection, Cornish Studies Library, Redruth)

He was disliked by staff and pupils, and found himself in trouble on account of chewing the sheets of his dormitory bed. He was passive, not aggressive, and when bullied offered no resistance and never retaliated. He told lies just for the sake of it, and his school report of 1940 said, 'He ought still to be in the nursery.' He had been described as untidy, scruffy, grubby and lazy, and 'deserved harder treatment'. He was removed from Rugby because they could not cope with this 'very abnormal boy', and this was when he was introduced to the psychiatrist's couch. Having failed to fit in at one boarding school, he was destined to be placed in another, Blundell's at Tiverton, which was rather nearer home, but where he also remained an outsider.

When Dr Craig, a psychiatrist, examined Miles in 1940, he was struck with the blueness of his extremities, his expressionless face, his dullness and apathy, lack of emotion and insight. Craig learned from Mr and Mrs Giffard that Miles was an habitual liar, and that he suffered from violent night terrors and sudden panic attacks for no apparent reason. He was by nature somewhat timid and cringing, being anxious to avoid struggles or violence. The doctor diagnosed Miles as a juvenile schizophrenic with a psychopathic personality, living in a dream world at one moment and in reality at the other. This would subsequently be thought to be responsible for him not knowing at the time of the killing that what he was doing was wrong. He was said to be in a state of clouded conscience. His condition in 1940 was sufficiently serious for him to be taken back to Cornwall and given treatment by one of Dr Craig's assistants. Then arrangements were made for him to receive treatment three times a fortnight at Blundell's, which unfortunately made him miss games, the only thing at which he excelled. When the psychiatrist had first suspected schizophrenia, the hereditary factor had seemed to be missing. But everything clicked into place four years later, when Mr Giffard sought a consultation for a second breakdown, mental breakdowns being considered akin to schizophrenia. According to the psychiatrist, his fears were rooted in early childhood, when a sadistic nanny had beaten him severely and locked him in a cupboard.

Dr Craig had decided to stop the treatment after two years, fearing that further attempts to ease the difficulties deep down in his mind could precipitate an acute outburst, causing an enormous amount of damage. They had got the patient 'superficially better'. He did not consider that Miles had ever been normal mentally, and had warned his general practitioner and his parents that he could have a schizophrenic episode at any time. Defective reasoning and judgment were both cardinal symptoms. Miles had suffered a period of remission from 1943 to 1947 whilst in the Navy, breaking down and getting progressively worse from then on. In view of all this Dr Craig was not surprised to hear of what had apparently transpired in 1952.

Dr Rossiter Lewis, a Harley Street psychiatrist and former prison medical officer who had seen Miles on three occasions, said that at the time of the murders he was suffering from a defect of reason due to a disease of the mind. At the time of these violent acts, he had known what he was doing to some extent, but had not known that he was doing wrong either in the moral sense or in the sense of being against the law. Tests had shown that apart from having a schizoid personality Miles had a defect of sugar in the blood, which could affect the brain, giving rise to sudden impulsive outbursts, impairment of judgment, grossly irresponsible behaviour and no appreciation of right or wrong.

The medical evidence for the defence had been very compelling. But Dr Hood, the Giffards' family doctor, who was a medical witness for the Crown, projected another view, from an entirely different perspective. He said that after the cruel nurse left, the boy was completely normal. 'He was a bright, cheery little chap, and I never observed any sign of abnormality in him.' Hood had known about the night terrors, and, although *he* had referred Miles to the psychiatrist in the first place, he said he had no recollection of Dr Craig emphasising any deep-seated mental trouble. He said that Miles had been a disappointment to his father, an 'idle little waster', and mentioned him being drunk at a Hunt Ball. Dr Matheson, principal medical officer at Brixton Prison, another prosecution witness, had had Miles under his scrutiny and carried out various tests during the time he was in prison. He did not consider Miles to be a schizophrenic. He agreed that he may have experienced hallucinations and panic attacks as a child, but attached no importance to this, saying that children often had disproportionate reactions to trivial things. He was dismissive of all the evidence given by the defence.

Throughout the trial Miles had shown very little interest and seemed devoid of emotion as he sat between two warders. During his summing up the judge said 'the man who butchered Mr and Mrs Giffard, if he is not protected by being insane in law, is a murderer.' It took the jury just 35 minutes to return a verdict of 'Guilty'. When Mr Justice Oliver sentenced him to death he added 'And may God have mercy on your soul,' and Miles was heard to murmur, 'Amen'.

There was great concern about this verdict, and five submissions were made to the Home Secretary, including one from a French-born female member of the jury, who was convinced that Miles was insane. General Sir George Giffard supplied confidential family information about his abnormalities since his nursery days; the headmaster of Blundell's School described his disturbed schooldays; an eminent Harley Street psychiatrist, who was a recognised authority on mental illness and its relation to crime, stressed the importance of considering the condemned man's mental history; concerned members of the public contributed statements about his disturbed state of mind. But this was to no avail. Miles was hanged at Bristol prison eighteen days later.

THE RUSBRIDGER
RIDDLE

On the face of it, the man who came to live in a handsome little cottage in a hamlet near Bodmin in the mid-1970s seemed to have enjoyed a dashing, colourful lifestyle, travelling to exotic foreign cities and experiencing the sort of vibrant adventures that most of us can only dream of. Friends and journalists calling at his cottage in Tremorebridge might enjoy smoked salmon sandwiches and a glass or two of Chablis and marvel at James Rusbridger's wonderful tales concerning his days as a spy, when he acted as a bagman in Eastern Europe. Although he was often alone, people found him charming, well mannered and interesting company. He had a number of influential close friends who cared deeply about him and his welfare. In recent years he had been experiencing stress-related health problems following a series of overwhelming financial setbacks and the death of his mother. So his neighbours were very concerned when they noticed that his curtains remained drawn on the morning of 16th February 1994, and contacted his landlord, who lived nearby.

On 17th February the St Blazey and Par edition of the *Cornish Guardian* inserted a small report on the front page to the effect that police had been called to a cottage at Tremorebridge, where a man was found hanging. At the time of going to press the police were still at the scene, together with the district coroner. They would not confirm the identity of the man, who was believed to be a local writer. Other editions of the paper bore the headline

'AUTHOR HANGED' and stated that the man, James Rusbridger, was a well known writer of letters to the local and national press and the author of three books concerned with espionage. He was related to Peter Wright of *Spycatcher* fame and had worked in the intelligence services. The *Cornish Guardian* also made mention of his conviction for defrauding a local company of about £3,000 some three years previously, after he had suffered a mental breakdown. He had subsequently attempted suicide and was later acquitted on a shoplifting charge in St Austell.

The *Western Morning News* of 17th February, however, had a feature on the 'kinky death' riddle of the secret service agent James Rusbridger and reproduced a striking photograph of him, looking quizzical, yet knowing. It went on to explain that the former MI6 agent was found hanged on the day he was due to be evicted from his cottage because of huge rent arrears. His shocked landlord had discovered him hanging in ropes suspended from the loft and surrounded by pornographic pictures, video tapes and a variety of documents. Nationwide newspapers then picked up the story and carried reports of his chilling departure from this world, trussed up in a chemical warfare suit, with overalls, plastic macintosh, long black boots, rubber gloves, gasmask and a sou'wester, and wild rumours flew about all over the place. Some sought to find a connection between his subversive activities after leaving the secret service and the weird manner of his passing; some thought that his cottage was being bugged; some thought that he was being blackmailed. Others regarded him as a fraud, with his kinky death the result of perverted sexual activities which had got out of hand. Indeed, the day before his apparent suicide he had submitted an article entitled 'Pornography and the Public' to an associate on a London newspaper – this included seedy details of the bizarre death a week before, on 8th February, of Stephen Milligan MP, a death to which his own was to bear such a remarkable resemblance.

Nevertheless tributes poured in from shocked friends, who only wished that they could turn the clock back, and minister to him in his time of despair. They spoke of the invaluable work he had done in exposing embarrassing governmental cover-ups. Journalists and other media personalities who had enjoyed his company and been drawn into his complex world of conspiracy and Whitehall

James Rusbridger. (*Western Morning News*)

double-dealing produced reverential potted histories depicting a glamorous career, which almost threatened to out-Bond James Bond himself. The media had seen him as the perfect spy, a source of sensitive information that was not available elsewhere. This close relationship had enabled reporters to build up a profile of James Rusbridger and his exciting lifestyle.

According to these biographical accounts, James Rusbridger was born in Jamaica in 1928, the third child of a colonel in the Duke of Wellington's regiment. The family returned to Aldershot when he was three, and his pleasant singing voice gained him a place at a choir school before he went on to Dover College. He was always fascinated with gadgetry and, after completing his national service, he took a course in draughtsmanship. Then a brief spell working in the Naval Design Office at Vickers Armstrong involved him in the testing of a variety of post-war naval weapons.

A successful application for a job advertised in the *Daily Telegraph* in 1952, when he was 24, gave him the chance to design a sugar refinery. This opened up some promising opportunities for advancement overseas and to make some influential international contacts. Impressed by his acumen, his employers sent him off on a sugar marketing course which led to the opening of an office in London for a Cuban sugar company.

As the managing director of a company dealing with an international commodity, he was well placed to manipulate the market to political ends. While on a trip to New York, Rusbridger claimed to have been approached by the CIA, with a plot to destabilise Fidel Castro by deflating Cuban sugar prices. His cynical response was to nominate a fee so outrageous that they would back off, but to his astonishment they paid up, and thus the international political scene was shaken by sugar.

Rusbridger's association with MI6 supposedly began in 1962, when the Foreign Office approached him to act as a courier. Throughout the 1960s he cut quite a dash in and out of the Army and Navy Club in Piccadilly. Stealthy contact officers devised a number of dark and daring assignments for him, whereby parcels containing thousands of dollars would be smuggled into Eastern Europe in return for vital documents. This he accomplished in the guise of a sophisticated businessman, driving ostentatiously through the streets of Prague and Warsaw in an E-type Jaguar. Then, in 1974, he left this lucrative lifestyle of high class international business and double dealing to establish himself in Cornwall, firstly at St Austell and then in a little hamlet to the west of Bodmin.

James Rusbridger's retirement to Cornwall must have been quite a culture shock. The reduction in his circumstances proved hard to cope with, and he soon ran into financial difficulties. He took a job as a stock control manager at a local cash and carry store, where he found himself in trouble after irregularities were discovered in the stock, and he was placed on probation for two years.

Over the last twenty years of his life he poured his energies into controversial writing, criticising the Establishment in general, and the security services in particular. He bombarded the local and national press with letters about intelligence matters, royalty, the Second World War, and complex webs of intrigue and conspiracy. He wrote a characteristically mischievous letter to the *Western Morning News*, published on the day of his death, demanding to know how the Devon and Cornwall police could afford to build their new firing range if they did not have the money to put

Jasmin Cottage, Tremorebridge, where James Rusbridger was found hanged in 1994. (Taken with kind permission of David Harris)

policemen on the beat. His article on pornography had been sent off to another newspaper at the same time.

His first book *The Intelligence Game*, published in 1989, sought to uncover the dirty tricks of intelligence services such as the CIA, KGB and MI5. In *Who Sank Surcouf?*, published in 1991, he uncovered the bungled sinking of a French submarine by the Americans during the war. *Betrayal at Pearl Harbour,* which Rushbridger co-authored was also published in 1991 and claimed that London had advance warning of the Japanese attack on Pearl Harbour, which Churchill refused to act upon. As he became more widely known as an informed commentator, his expertise was increasingly in demand with the media, particularly makers of documentaries.

Within a day or two of deferential tributes appearing in some of the country's leading newspapers, there was a sudden backlash. Well-known experts in the field of espionage were casting doubts on his credibility, saying that anyone with inside knowledge could pick out flaws and inaccuracies in his accounts and that he had never been employed by the British intelligence services. The reality, they claimed, was that he was a fantasist, who had been fooling publishers and the media for years and his death was worthy of one of his more contrived plots. 'His death was as much a fantasy as his life,' said one expert, and he poured scorn on the very notion of driving an E-type Jaguar through Prague in 1962 – adding that even Bond's creator would have considered that a little too far fetched. Senior intelligence officers' categorical denials that he had ever had any connection with any branch of British intelligence appeared in every national newspaper. On 24th February the *Western Morning News* reported that Whitehall insisted that he had never been a member of the security or secret services. So was this the spy who never was?

If Rusbridger's death had sparked off a national controversy about spies being left out in the cold, or spies who never-had-been, the inquest at Bodmin threw more light on an obscure situation. In short, it concluded that the 65 year old man with bondage and asphyxia fetishes had taken his own life in what appeared to have been a bizarre attempt to upstage the notorious death of Stephen Milligan. The coroner recorded a verdict of suicide, and said that it had either been a case of accidental asphyxiation, or a deliberate act calculated to attract the utmost publicity and out-Milligan Milligan. The pathologist revealed that the cause of death had been asphyxia due to hanging. At the inquest on Stephen Milligan it had been decided that he had been indulging in a sexual practice which went wrong, when he was discovered with a plastic bag over his head and a cord around his neck, and a verdict of misadventure was thus returned.

Rusbridger's body had been found at his cottage suspended by a rope around his neck extending down to his crotch through a system of shackles. There were ropes round his legs and ankles, and there was a padlocked chain around his waist. He was apparently obsessed with Milligan, although they had never met. It later transpired that he once had to be released from a garden shed, after getting trapped there as a result of over-enthusiastic, self-inflicted sado-masochistic adventures.

Those who knew him may have been surprised by Rusbridger's strange style of departure, but not by his apparent decision to take his own life, for he had become increasingly overwhelmed by financial problems in recent months and increasingly depressed, and had spoken of suicide. In fact, he had told people that the age of 65 would be a good time to go. Police found a letter making it clear that he intended to take his own life. If there were any rumours still flying about concerning conspiratorial plots, reds under beds, bugs in jugs, spies in the skies or a mole up the pole, it was made quite plain that no one else was involved in the death of this unhappy man. What happened was clearly the result of his own actions. The coroner cut a swath through all the complex clutter by declaring, 'There is less to this than meets the eye!' And one admiring commentator was heard to mutter, 'Now Rusbridger is dead, long live non-conspiracy!'

Bibliography

Barton, R.M., *Life in Cornwall*, Vols 1, 2, 3, & 4
Canner, A.C., *The Parish of Tintagel*
Davison, Brian K., *Tintagel Castle*
Hocking, Dr F.D.M., *Bodies and Crimes, A Pathologist Speaks*
Hunt, Robert, *Popular Romances of the West of England*
Perry, Ronald, Royal Institution of Cornwall Journal, 1999, *Silvanus Trevail & the Development of Modern Tourism in Cornwall*
Saffron, Cheryl, *Pagan Cornwall, Land of the Goddess*
Taylor, William, *The History of Tintagel*
Whetter, James, Cornish Banner, Nov 1993, No 74, *Silvanus Trevail, Architect*

All England Law Reports, Vol 2, 1944

Cornish Guardian
The Cornish Post & Mining News & Redruth Advertiser
Falmouth Packet
The Guardian & Gazette
The Royal Cornwall Gazette & Cornwall County News
The Times
West Briton
West Briton & Cornwall Advertiser
Western Morning News

Acknowledgements

With grateful thanks to the following for their assistance:
Bodmin Town Museum
Cornish Studies Library, The Cornwall Centre
Cornwall Archaeological Unit, Truro
English Heritage
Falmouth Library
Housel Bay Hotel

Police Museum, Middlemoor, Exeter
Royal Cornwall Museum
Shire Hall, Bodmin
Truro Library

David Harris, Derek & Freda Oswald, Simon Parker,
Carl Thorpe

Photographs by the author unless stated otherwise